Release Your Writing

Book Publishing, *Your* Way

♦ Helen Gallagher
Author of *Computer Ease*

Cover design & collage by Peg Miller
pegmiller@nehalemtel.net

"Release Your Writing," by Helen Gallagher.
ISBN 978-1-60264-060-3.

Library of Congress Control Number on file with Publisher.

Manufactured in the United States of America.

Table of Contents

Attract a publisher if you can, but if not, don't _wait_ your life away....

Publish your book yourself.

Introduction

Whether you're a writer just starting out or you're finishing a book, you *can* get your work published.

You know the long road to publishing success: attract an agent who has time and connections to place your book with a publisher, and follow the slow journey to publication. But there is another way: publish it yourself!

This book explores traditional publishing and offers strategies for success with self-publishing, putting you in control of the process.

But what about the writing itself, and managing computer files, and formatting a book for publication? How does an author handle marketing and promotion? We'll take you there too. *Release Your Writing* walks you through the whole process, not just publishing options, and is based on extensive research publishing my own books as well as advising clients on the best route to successful and timely publication.

1

Why self-publish? Perhaps ...

- ❏ You want your work to be seen. No one can read what's in your desk drawer.
- ❏ You want to help people with what you've learned, and share your expertise.
- ❏ You have a collection of essays or stories you'd like to sell.
- ❏ You want a book for professional reasons, as an adjunct to your business.
- ❏ You've studied the markets and you know you aren't likely to attract a major publisher...

Then self-publishing might be perfect for you.

When I wrote *Computer Ease,* to celebrate my tenth business anniversary, I wanted it on the market for the December 2005 holiday sales season. Working back from that deadline, I had to get on the publisher's schedule for early October. August and September were consumed by all the important final revisions plus editing, cover design and the book's front and back matter. My publisher, Virtual Bookworm, Inc., took care of the rest. *Computer Ease* is still enjoying life, as "the book that won't beep, crash, or call you a dummy." Bringing it to life and enjoying book-signing parties is a marvelous reward for the effort. *Computer Ease* was chosen by Forbes Book Club, won a non-fiction award from Illinois Women's Press Association, and still sells well... because I believed in the project, and I got it out there.

Release Your Writing presumes no strong computer skills and recognizes not everyone writes with a computer. Yet technology does lend a hand if you compose and edit your work via computer and need to format a manuscript for publication. You'll learn techniques for manuscript management and revision. Even advanced computer users will find time-saving techniques, formatting tricks, ways to polish documents, and manage the business of writing.

Release Your Writing moves you toward getting your work published, whether a benevolent agent/publisher relationship is around the corner, or you have the time and money to fund the publishing process. Most of all, it offers you a strategy for preparing your manuscript and getting your book published through print-on-demand (POD), a technology becoming more and more embraced by the book industry. Authors are learning they can realize success with their book, control the process and keep the profits.

So let's get started on publishing your book, *your* way.

Part 1

Getting Published

Chapter 1

A Changing Publishing Industry

Publishing as an industry has grown by almost 17 percent per year since 2005, and net revenues for all books are projected to top $40.4 billion by 2010, according to The Book Industry Study Group in New York. A few companies, just five or six, control over 80 percent of the industry. Most books in bookstores come from those few firms. Only one to two percent of unsolicited submissions are purchased for publication. That's why self-publishing and print-on-demand (POD) are projected to show continued growth and why they've gained acceptance as valid publishing choices.

Let's take a brief look at traditional publishing methods, before we launch into publishing *your* way.

For traditional publishing, an agent is considered essential to present your manuscript to publishers and negotiate the best deal. That's what they do best. In return, most agents earn about a 15 percent fee on your advance and future sales. Publishers prefer to work through agents because of their expertise, so most won't even look at unagented manuscripts.

Agents' work is not unlike the real estate business, in that there is an agent, a buyer, and a seller. An agent won't take your book on unless he or she believes it has a chance of being sold. Agents do not make money representing you until you make money.

Scout the market for agents who might represent you, use your contacts for referrals and track likely publishers. Don't overlook small and regional publishers if that fits your niche. Then sit down with one of these good books on how to write a book proposal and put your best writing into the proposal.

Even though self-publishing is changing some of the old rules, knowledge about book proposals will help you organize and target your writing.

Consult:

- Jeff Herman's *Write the Perfect Book Proposal: 10 That Sold and Why,* and

- Susan Rabiner's *Thinking Like Your Editor: How to Write Great Serious Nonfiction-and Get It Published,* and

- *Book Proposals That Sell* by W. Terry Whalin.

Book Proposal

If you want to attract a traditional publisher, a book proposal is the most important writing project you'll undertake. Agents generally want to see sample chapters rather than a proposal for fiction. For non-fiction, if you go the traditional publishing route, you will need a formal book proposal to submit to agents, who can determine how marketable your book is. I do know people who sell a book without a proposal, but for the long journey to a publishing contract, the proposal helps make sure you put in your research time, study the market and focus your approach and get the best possible contract.

A book proposal includes, at a minimum:

1. Table of contents
2. Synopsis and chapter outline: This is a valuable exercise even if you're not doing a formal proposal. It solidifies in your mind not just the topic, but your spin. What makes your viewpoint original, unique, important?
3. Sample chapters (usually two).
4. Your background and credibility to write the book.
5. Target market: Who is your audience? The tighter you define your ideal reader, the easier it is for an agent or editor to position your book.
6. Competitive analysis, showing how your book differs from others on the market.
7. Marketing and promotion: Specify the marketing effort you're willing to handle. Mention any prior radio and TV exposure.

Getting published may not be a good use of your time, if it means shopping for an agent, writing a lengthy proposal, and waiting to sell it to a publisher. And, the road to rejection can be quite long. Do you want to wait six months to get a "No, thank you," from a publisher? Unless you've already been published and have an agent to represent you, your chances of selling a book to a publisher are extremely low.

Traditional publishers excel at their marketing knowledge and distribution. Those are the two primary areas where a new writer will benefit from using a traditional publisher. If you write a best-seller, yes, you, your agent and your publisher will reap profits for years, but most of the advice in this book enlightens writers about other ways of achieving publishing success, instead of waiting for the Publishing Gods to send for us.

Looking Beyond Top Publishers

Just as independent bookstores serve a different niche than national book retailers, so too do smaller publishers. Even large publishing companies try various imprints, small in-house brands aimed at specific markets. HarperCollins has several imprints, such as Ecco, launched for classic literature, and Fourth Estate for edgy fiction and non-fiction. Some publishers are now collapsing their imprints back into one brand, noting they create clutter and confusion.

Small presses are big business in America. This includes university, regional and independent firms. Small presses comprise a huge part of the book industry, over 80,000 firms. The Jenkins Group, Inc. reports that small and self-produced books represent 78 percent of all titles. Learn more about small presses at IndependentPublisher.com. Many small publishers are willing to work with authors, even unagented, and tend to keep books in print longer than larger firms. Of course, your book can still be remaindered or rejected for a second print run if sales don't meet the publisher's goals.

Do your homework before approaching publishers. Look at their website or their book catalogs. Does your book match up with their style? Can you find those books in your local stores? What is their distribution channel? What are their contract provisions for keeping your book in print? Do their authors retain the rights to their work? What marketing support is available? These are usually called co-op fees, where the publisher *might* fund local marketing events with postcards or promotional items tied to your book's theme.

While a publisher's advance and the promise of royalties hold allure, royalties, often in the range of 2 to 12 percent aren't paid to the author until the publisher makes back the advance. So even on a small advance of $5,000 it will be a long time before you begin receiving a percentage of sales. If your book is a best seller, you can move to an island off Crete. For the rest of us, there are other options we'll explore in depth.

Publishers generally expect projects to sell at eight to ten times the cost of production. Their gross profit pays for a full editorial staff, design team, and a big marketing budget. A publisher's goal is to produce a book that gives them a nice net profit. After all, they are taking most of the financial risk. For most authors, it's a tough way to make money, so other publishing options start to look pretty good.

Most books need to sell a minimum of 1,200 copies to be considered a marginal success in the publishing world and over 7,000 copies to sustain interest. If you hand-sell and reach 600 copies, or 800, are you a failure? Is your book a flop? No, because you can keep selling your book as long as you wish.

Publishers make sales estimates based on tight marketing budgets, cash flow needs, and calendars of new books coming along. Only you can sustain interest in your own work. The traditional publishing method hasn't changed in over 100 years, and leaves something to be desired in the 21st century. Bookstores keep books on the shelf only a few months, drop them if they don't sell and return unsold merchandise, regardless of condition.

Here's the view of Nolan Lewis, author of *Clouds are Always White on Top,* from a recent online forum for the Chicago Writer's Association, ChicagoWrites.org:

> "My book sells for $28.95 in hard cover. My take is $1.73 per book. And that is a normal royalty. I spent years on it. The publisher spends a few weeks, possibly. The book distributor probably never sees the book, just the invoices and he wants 15 percent. The bookstore spends minutes on this particular book and takes 40 percent, and wants it on consignment so he has no gamble. Something's wrong here."

With a traditional publishing contract, a publisher can allow a book to go out of print, or refuse to do a second print run. By self-publishing, your book is never out of print. People can order as little as one copy and your POD firm handles the order, requesting the digital press produce the book, usually overnight. You can order any quantity, at a large discount, for resale.

If you have a book that's gone out of print with a publisher, check your contract and see if you have the right to reprint it yourself or with another publisher. iUniverse is one POD firm that has a special program for reviving out-of-print books.

> Who believes in your book? You do. Who decides if your book will be a best-seller? Only your readers. And what's the best way to get your book to the market? Publish it yourself.

Book Structure—The Whole Package

What do you need to put a book together?

1. A good manuscript in digital format, produced on computer.

2. Cover design—A bad cover won't necessarily kill book sales, but a good cover can make a big difference in sales. If a reader takes your book off the shelf, on average, he or she will gaze at the cover about four seconds and then flip the book over to read the back cover, for about seven seconds. So you don't have much time to win them over.

3. Title page—start with a working title, but don't make a firm decision until you run it by several people, and look up the title in search engines. Are you in good company? Book titles can't be copyrighted but it is doubtful you'd want to use a title that's easily confused with another book. Another important consideration is the length of the title. What looks good on the cover may be a poor choice on the book's spine. The spine has to be readable to urge a book browser to pick it up.

4. Front matter—Your publisher will set up the pages preceding the actual

book text. Items include the inner title page with ISBN, copyright notice, and publication information.

5. Back cover—Generally includes author photo, promotional copy, endorsements.

6. Table of Contents—not usually necessary for fiction.

7. A foreword or introduction.

8. Chapters.

9. Back matter—resources, references, index, link to your website.

10. Acknowledgments.

Later, Chapter 7, Computer Power Tools, will help you create and manage these book components.

Know The Market
When you think of a book you've really enjoyed, what held your interest? You don't need to emulate other writers, but you should identify what makes a compelling and engaging experience for your readers.

If you have a series of essays or columns you want to turn into a book, study successful essay collections and authors you admire. A common mistake is compiling a book from unrelated pieces. That's exactly what it will be: A collection of disparate articles. Think about what could make it cohesive. Read widely and see what holds good collections together.

When writing a book proposal or your book, be sure to visit the library and several bookstores, both chains and independent. See what other books are in your category. How will you compare? What's the price range for those books? What kind of depth do they have? Is the category so large that you'll be lost in it?

When I wrote *Computer Ease,* a trip to the bookstore was the final step convincing me to self-publish. In chain stores, the computer section was full of 400-page technical manuals and how-to books for very narrow niches. In independent bookstores, there is no computer section. *Computer Ease* is different. It shares the philosophy and humor of coping with computers, with some serious hands-on help included. It would never be shelved or found by my target audience if it was stocked with computer how-to books.

Chapter 2

Self-publishing

As the industry changes and gains respectability, self-publishing is promoted by organizations that wouldn't have considered it just two or three years ago. *Writer's Digest* magazine has an annual self-published book award, and an issue devoted to self-publishing and *The Writer* magazine runs articles on self-publishing success. The American Society of Journalists & Authors (ASJA) recently broadened membership criteria to include some self-published books, and has partnered with a print-on-demand (POD) firm.

Getting your book published is within your reach.
I frequently hear people say: "I will probably self-publish if I can't get a publisher." Yet, self-publishing is not settling for second best. It's the right choice if your book won't likely capture the attention of a large publisher and you don't want to spend years waiting to see your book in print.

In fact, many self-published authors do attract a traditional publisher, once their book is a success, so you're not closing any doors by publishing your own books. Authors such as Margaret Atwood, Steven King, Jack Canfield and Deepak Chopra chose self-publishing, even after a long successful career with traditional publishing companies.

We often hear why self-published books and POD are a bad idea: No agent to represent you, no bookstore distribution. We rarely hear why it's a good idea. You control the production process, cover, pricing and marketing, you can still get agent representation, and your book need never go out of print.

Several mainstream publishers made news recently, promoting the self-publishing and POD concept.

- Hyperion president Bob Miller said: "We try to keep a book in print as long as possible, and print-on-demand now makes that easier than ever before."

- The POD firm Xlibris is a strategic partner of Random House. Amazon owns BookSurge, and Barnes & Noble owns iUniverse.

There are two primary types of self-publishing. It can mean "the works," where you design and typeset the book, pay out-of-pocket to have thousands of copies printed and delivered to your care. You personally fulfill and ship all orders, receive payment, and do all bookkeeping. Or self-publishing can mean print-on-demand, which is much easier.

If you choose true self-publishing, you can create your own entity, such as Sunny Street Publishing. You're in charge of the entire production process, finding an editor, a cover designer, obtaining ISBNs (defined below), and getting the book printed to your specifications. You choose the binding, paper weight, cover layout, make page formatting decisions, and order a large enough print-run to be cost-effective. Since you may be ordering 3,000 books, you have to make sure all those details are perfect.

Print-on-demand is the second type of self-publishing, which we'll explore shortly.

Manuscript Editing

Beyond the mechanics of word processing, which we'll cover below, allow plenty of time for high-quality editing. Not using a traditional publishing firm means you forgo the expertise of a salaried editor laboring over your grammar, punctuation, and every turn of phrase. Expert editing is a requirement for your book if you self-publish. Unless you've made a career as an editor, you'll have to pay for professional editing or perhaps trade for in-kind services.

To find a good editor, check *The Writer* and *Writer's Digest,* or ask other authors for a recommendation. They work is not cheap and it shouldn't be. Read that last sentence again. That's exactly the kind of mistake you might not catch. As I said... Their work is not cheap and it shouldn't be. It's essential. Some self-publishing firms will edit your book for an added fee, but make inquiries to be sure it is high-quality editing, not just spelling and punctuation.

As a self-published entity, while your book is being printed, you arrange for warehouse storage, and find a distributor. A distributor acts as middleman, handling inventory, warehousing and getting the book to retail outlets. Their reps visit book buyers to show catalogs and take orders. And that costs money. Most proponents of full self-publishing tout the low cost per book, yet offset print costs, distributor fees and the value of your time all add up.

And while you *can* format the book in your word processing program, you don't want the finished copy to look like plain vanilla text. If you don't have an eye for it, you'll pay someone to format your manuscript for chapter headings, callout boxes, graphics, sub-heads, and a table of contents.

Self-publishing is not a license to produce a book that isn't your best work, or a first effort that really isn't ready to be published. Give yourself time, and like any craft, study, practice, and improve your editing and writing.

When you manage the publishing process, you own every copy and need a bank merchant account for credit card sales, shipping, recordkeeping, inventory storage and tracking. You'll spend a lot on mailing costs and give away a lot of books, maybe 50 or 100 to get reviews and publicity. Once you have the inventory, you're pretty much committed to getting steady sales to recover your costs.

The downside of this type of self-publishing includes:

1. You may need a large cash outlay.
2. Too often, self-published books look unprofessional.
3. It's hard to get reviewed, because there is an impression that self-published books are not well edited, and publications like *The Wall Street Journal* or *Woman's Day* won't review a book that isn't available through retail channels.
4. It can take a long time to make back your investment.

Getting Help and Advice

Successful self-publishers are a generous breed. If you pursue this route you'll encounter many people able to offer advice and help you make sense of the choices.

You'll find a wealth of self-publishing resources at Jacqueline Simonds' site at Creative Minds Press, www.creativemindspress.com/newbiefaq.htm. Her firm offers book-packaging services including editing, layout and design. Know what you're getting into before you choose self-publishing. Your book will only stay alive as long as you have the time and resources to manage and promote it.

The Independent Book Publishers Association, pma-online.org, has a trade distribution program to aid member authors/publishers who do not have bookstore distribution. For a fee, currently $55, PMA can evaluate your book for possible acceptance in a distribution program. There may be a distribution commission beyond the evaluation fee.

Another avenue for self-published authors is a consignment wholesaler, but as with PMA's trade distribution program, it's not without cost. These avenues make sense if you have a large inventory and feel your book will sustain sales in the thousands.

If self publishing sounds right for you, SPAN, the Small Publishers Association of North America, (www.spannet.org) can put you in touch with just about every resource you'd need, and with self-publishers who are willing to share their experiences.

And Dan Poynter posts a full list of suppliers for self-publishing projects at parapublishing.com/sites/para/resources/supplier.cfm

Distribution

Self-published authors have to work at getting distribution. Think beyond traditional retail bookstores and consider some less obvious markets for sales. Market a book about wine to area wine shops, and ethnic cook books to travel shops. The national store chain Anthropologie has a wonderfully esoteric book selection in a very offbeat retail shop.

Distributors are also the secret to getting your book into airport shops around the country. Two top airport bookstore retailers are Hudson Booksellers and The Paradies Shops. Hudson operates over 400 newsstands in airports and train stations. Paradies has a unique "Read & Return" program where travelers can purchase a book to read and return it within six months for a 50 percent credit. You can reach them through distribution companies such as Bookazine, Anderson

News or Midpoint. See the Appendix for full contact information.

Copyright Protection
You automatically own the copyright to anything you produce. Copyright lasts for seventy years after death, after which works become public domain. A good intellectual property attorney will help you plan for transfer of your book's rights so they don't fall into public domain. If you publish through a traditional publisher or use print-on-demand, the copyright is registered for you. If you self-publish in the U.S., you need to mail two copies of your book to the Library of Congress for official recording of the copyright. Many authors also mail a copy of the book to themselves, leaving it in a sealed envelope with postmark, as further proof.

Learn more at loc.gov/copyright. Yes, snail mail is archaic. The U.S. copyright office is now beta-testing an electronic copyright filing procedure.
www.copyright.gov/eco/beta-announce.html

Don't confuse copyright with an ISBN registration (below). You own the copyright to your work the minute you write it. Registering the copyright with the Library of Congress (www.loc.gov) proves you are the author.

What is an ISBN?
The International Standard Book Number is a unique number assigned to every book published. It identifies the publisher and is used for inventory control. ISBNs are sold in a minimum bundle of ten numbers. As of this writing, the cost is $240 plus processing fees. All ISBN's are issued by R.R. Bowker LLC (www.isbn.org).

If you're self-publishing just one or two books, you can avoid the expense of buying ten numbers, since a POD firm will use one of their ISBNs, and include the cost as part of your publishing fee. They probably buy a thousand at a time. But if you plan to be in the publishing business full time, or plan a series of books, owning the ISBN yourself may suit you. If you publish multiple books or publish your book in multiple formats, (softcover, hardcover, CD, DVD, ebook, audio book) each needs its own ISBN.

Until recently, ISBNs were ten-digit numbers, and are now expanded to 13 digits. The first few digits of an ISBN identify the country and publisher. If your publishing plans are ambitious, buy either the minimum ten, or the next size block, which is 100, so the publisher prefix remains the same for all the works you produce.

In the 13-digit format, the first three digits, usually 978, are the group prefix, followed by codes for country, publisher, title and final check digit.

If the big unknown publishing factor is holding you back, explore self-publishing options today and release your writing.

Chapter 3

The POD Segment

For self-publishing without the heavy lifting, look to an affordable, high-quality POD firm to print your manuscript, help with cover design, make it available for sale on all the major online book-selling sites, and handle orders. You'll find some POD firms overpriced and short on quality, so it's essential that you do your homework before choosing a publisher.

POD firms are <u>not</u> what used to be called vanity press. Those firms charged high fees, paid no royalties, and took all your rights.

POD is digital printing, to produce books on demand in any quantity. POD books are "perfect-bound," a book binding technique using glue rather than stitches. Almost all trade paperbacks are perfect-bound. POD also refers to a distribution method of printing and shipping books to meet demand for orders.

POD books appear in online databases for immediate sales. These include the obvious: Amazon and BN.com, but also Powell's, Waldenbooks, Books-A-Million, and the Books In Print database at Bowkerlink.com. Not everyone shops at Amazon. People have their favorite resources, so spread your exposure far and wide.

You can purchase discounted copies of your book from your POD firm, to sell on your own. Large inventory is not an expense, and there aren't costs associated with shipping an entire print run to you or to a warehouse. Yet the cost per-book is higher than offset printing.

Digital doesn't mean only single copies though. You can order copies to use at a corporate workshop, or for a charity event, with special covers. POD isn't literally one copy at a time although it can fulfill an order for a single book. It's also for short print runs, such as when a bookseller or library order several copies, when you need 100 copies for a conference, or if you get a special order for a large quantity. My POD firm, Virtual Bookworm, Inc. offered to move to offset printing when Kinko's and Sam's Club were considering my first book. That would allow me to offer the book to them at a lower cost.

With typical self-publishing you may pay for a large print run, typically 1,000 to 5,000 books for a lower cost-per-book and you make back your cost as you sell them. And that takes a long time. You are either handling sales yourself or paying for distribution. That's when POD starts to look pretty good. Your costs for POD are often lower than typical self-publishing where you only earn money for the books you sell, not all that you print. While you pay a higher price-per-copy for POD books, your total cost is much lower than full self-publishing, so you need to recoup less cost before turning a profit.

With POD, you know your total cost going in and have no further expense with the publisher. Quantities are printed as orders are placed and you share the profits of those sales.

Your share of profits comes to you as royalties on all copies sold, except those you buy at a reduced price for resale. You receive sales reports and when royalties reach a minimum level, usually $25 or $50, you receive a check. Some POD firms pay monthly, others are slow, with royalties calculated at the end of the quarter and then paid within sixty days. That's a five-month delay.

Royalties are based on a book's price. A good POD firm lets you determine the selling price, based on your market, not their desired profit. It's important, especially with POD and self-publishing, that you have control over the price. After analyzing the market, you know the price of comparable books, and you know your target audience, so set the price to fit the market.

From your first month as a POD author, you earn a royalty on sales. Host an event where you do back-of-the-room sales and you might sell 40 books in one day. If you purchased those copies from the publisher, you won't earn royalties because you got them at a discounted price, but you keep 100 percent of the sales price.

With self-publishing, if you print 3,000 copies of your book at $4.00 to get a good price on the print run, you're out $12,000 until you sell enough books to recoup your cost for printing, distribution and storage.

If you use POD, you pay a higher price per book, but pass that price on to the reader, exactly as mainstream publishers do when they sell a book at 70 percent over cost. They're making a profit and you should too.

We often hear of successful authors who publish through traditional publishers and never see a penny after their initial advance.

POD and ebooks (digital copies of print books) are just two examples of how publishing is changing. The traditional publishing industry, working the same way it did 100 years ago, may be scrambling to keep up. The lengthy time to production and low profit margins, in an industry awash in books means fewer people can enter the market. But POD and other formats open the gates of the publishing kingdom so a writer's work can be made available on an affordable and timely basis.

Is POD right for you? You will succeed with it if you write a good book and market it well. Focus on online exposure, local book-signing events, public speaking and offering your book to independent bookstores. These shops are usually very willing to support local authors, and we'll explore ways you can connect with them in Chapter 8.

Publishing Method Comparison

Feature	Traditional Publisher	Self-publishing	Print -on-demand
Control publishing process	No	Yes	Yes, through POD firm
Cost, excluding time	None	High	Low
Distribution	Yes	At your expense	Not wide distribution
Inventory management and storage	None	Full	None
ISBN in publisher's name	Yes	No	Yes
Life of book	May go out of print quickly	Can reprint at your expense	Stays in print forever
Marketing support	Little	Up to you	Up to you
Need a book proposal	Yes	No	No

Need agent representation	Yes	No	No
Need attorney to review contract	Yes	No	No
Need offer from publisher	Yes	No	No
Processing orders	Publisher's sales channel	You	POD firm
Publisher's advance	Likely	No	No
Royalties	Small, after advance earned back	None. You keep profit after ex-penses	Yes, 20-50 percent from first sale
Sales potential	Higher, through distributors	Lower, with you bearing all expense	High or low, depends on your effort
Timeframe	18 to 24 months	4 months	1-2 months
Unsold inventory	Returned for credit	Your burden	None

We've established that the POD process requires no long print run, no formidable lead-time, and no need to handle sales and shipping. Your POD vendor handles all the details of printing and sales. You pay an upfront fee for production and receive royalties on sales.

POD publishing and self-publishing are excellent ways to establish a market for your book, and even build the market to such an extent that you can sell the reprint rights to a much larger publisher for a good advance, if the book does well. Indeed, many larger publishers now scour the web for self-published and POD books that might fit their publishing program.

Choose POD ...

- ❑ If you want to control book production, timing and process: the content, title, cover, layout, and format.
- ❑ If you want your book to reach a targeted audience.
- ❑ If time matters. It can routinely take 12 to 18 months for a publisher to produce your manuscript. You can publish through POD in about six weeks.
- ❑ If you want 30 to 50 percent royalties instead of slow-drip publisher royalties averaging 2 to 12 percent.

The long route to an agent and publisher wasn't right for my needs when I published *Computer Ease*. My goal with the book, full of timely, current computer information, was to meet the immediate demand of my clients. Without the magical 'platform' required to attract the attention of a national publisher, I decided to write the book, create a cover, and choose a POD firm, Virtual Bookworm, Inc. After I submitted my manuscript electronically, and approved the final galleys, it appeared on major online retailer websites within three weeks. That's POD in a nutshell.

Publishing Statistics
> ➤ Only one to two percent of unsolicited submissions are purchased for publication.

> ➤ 95 percent of all books sell 7,500 copies or fewer.
> Source: EbookStand.com

With any publishing method, the marketing still falls to you. But don't worry; we have a plan for you to succeed with that too.

POD Book Production
We'll save the pep talk about technology for Chapter 6 but when it comes to preparing your manuscript, good computer skills will come in handy. Most POD

firms request online submission of all materials. In fact, some charge extra for snail mail. Once you sign a contract and submit your book components to the POD firm, the files remain on a computer ready to reprint with no setup costs and no large print run.

Basic submission files for manuscript assembly:

- Cover art, generally in separate file
- Bio and back cover text at end of main document
- Final table of contents and index included in the main document
- Chapter titles, font size, position on page and page margins follow publisher's guidelines
- If your book has images, send a separate list of images, by file name, and indicate page numbers for placement. Don't send poor quality images and hope they turn out okay. Learn how to adjust images and graphics (.jpg or .gif) for the required resolution (measured by dots-per-inch, .dpi).

You'll get galleys to proofread and then the actual printing process is pretty quick—even four to six weeks in some cases. POD usually offers very little editorial input so don't rush through the galleys. In fact, take the time to read them aloud. This is your last chance to fix any errors. Final quality is up to you. The publisher will send your first few books free, and at that time, it's already available for sale at Amazon, Barnes & Noble (bn.com) and scads of other online venues.

Your POD firm obtains the ISBN, creates a corresponding barcode, does the assembly and layout, and sends the file to Lightning Source to be printed. Lightning Source is the same printer used by most large publishers and is owned by Amazon. Self-published books account for 38 percent of their production.

Publishers Weekly industry statistics show Lightning Source prints about one million books per month. Not by coincidence, Lightning Source partners with Ingram Book Group, parent company of the wholesaler that supplies books to bookstores nationwide. Lightning Source also has a UK branch so your books will appear on amazon.uk and worldwide book selling sites as fast as in the US.

Ingram Book Group is the primary wholesaler used by bookstores. An order placed with Lightning Source before 6 PM will be in Ingram's warehouse by 4:30 AM. Ingram lists thousands of POD titles as "in inventory." Two years ago they used to show "delivery in three weeks." Technology has erased the disadvantage of slow turn-around printing for POD.

If your book needs extra work, you might wish to purchase additional editing or design services from your POD firm. Many of the services offered are tasks you can do yourself, so don't be eager to sign up for extra services at a fee. You might want to pay extra for cover artwork, or editorial services, but not for creating an index or table of contents, which you can easily do. Keep in mind, lack of editing and poor covers are generally cited as two primary reasons why self-published books don't sell well.

Standard Book Sizes

5 x 8 inches
5.5 x 8.5 inches
6 x 9 inches

The components of your book include the complete manuscript, cover art, a 150-200 word synopsis for the back cover and a 150-200-word author bio.

Production time varies, based on backlog and processing speed. If you want your book ready to coincide with a newsworthy event, plan ahead and ask your POD firm about their production schedule.

POD Printing
Is POD print quality as good as other publishing methods? Yes, largely because Lightning Source prints almost all books. They use high quality, acid-free, book-grade opaque paper stock. All books with trim sizes of 6"x9" or smaller are printed on a 55 lb. natural shade opaque. Larger books are printed on a 50 lb. white stock. Paperback covers are printed on a bright white 80 lb. cover stock. Almost all mainstream publishers and those who do traditional self-publishing get their books printed by this source.

Choosing a POD Firm

An author's reasons to use POD

- Need a limited number of books.
- Want to stay in print, not in a remainder bin.
- Desire to switch genres and maintain a presence with a different publisher.
- Target a special market or do co-branding with a nonprofit or corporate sponsor.
- Want a book as a promotional tool or workbook for classes and seminars.
- Want a sample chapter to distribute at seminars or workshops.
- Incentive to finish a book, knowing you can get it published.
- Want to be published and you aren't likely to attract an agent and publisher.
- Don't want to order thousands of books and have to manage distribution and order fulfillment.

Here is a list of just ten vendors, not inclusive, and subject to change. Use it to compare factors important to you, and then do further research on contract length and terms, copyright ownership, specific royalty terms, and time to market.

Beyond these basics, you'll want to check each vendor's website. Watch specifically for:

- What other books and categories they publish.
- How many books are in the "what's new" area.
- How easy their online order process is.
- Any special programs and promotions.

Publishing costs with POD depends on your appetite—softcover, hardcover, artwork, graphics, and of course number of pages. That determines ideal selling price although with most POD firms, you have the final say on price.

If you haven't seen a book published by the vendor you're considering, ask to see a sample, either hardcover or softcover. Some hardcover books by POD firms are case-bound with embossed lettering on the cover, instead of a traditional dust jacket.

If your book needs a dust jacket, or special features like a spiral-bound workbook or CD/DVD included, you might need to self-publish independently and use a book packager to manage the production of those components. Some POD firms limit their offerings to the most common book styles and sizes, to offer uniform pricing. You can always ask for pricing on special services and packaging.

When considering a POD firm, search Amazon.com to see what other books each publisher is selling. It's not a great sales measure, but check it out by clicking "Advanced Search" and inserting the publisher's name.

Finally, review the following chart. Evaluate what's important to you: costs, royalties, rights, etc. Visit vendor sites for more specific details. Most have a sample contract online. All of these contracts are more complex than portrayed here. Narrow down your choices and spend time analyzing POD vendors.

Ten POD firms (data verified at vendor sites)	Rates	Author discount	Royalties
AuthorHouse authorhouse.com Pays 60 days after quarter	$698+	40%	5-50% direct, 5-15% external
Booklocker booklocker.com Wants ebook exclusive Pays royalty monthly	$299+	35% and up	35% direct sales, 15%
BookSurge (owned by Amazon) booksurge.com Ala carte pricing	$499+	30%	25% list thru their channels, 10% other
Infinity Publishing infinitypublishing.com Check rights upon termi-nation	$499+	40-50% based on quantity	30% list 15% dist
iUniverse, Inc. (owned by Barnes & Noble) iuniverse.com They set retail price	$599+	30-35%	20-35% net
Llumina Press llumina.com Pays 60 days after quarter	$799	45%	30% list 10% dist
Outskirts Press Outskirtspress.com No sales thru their site	$200-1000/ varies	author decides	author decides
Virtual Bookworm virtualbookworm.com Pays royalty monthly	$360+ varies	30-50% based on quantity	50% net
Wheatmark Wheatmark.com Layout included in price	$799+	40-50%	40% direct, 20% external
Xlibris Corporation (owned by Random House), xlibris.com Custom templates	$499-1000	30%	25% soft, 10% dist

Like comparison-shopping for anything else, watch out for feature creep. Stick to the elements you know are important to you, and consider your overall budget before paying for extras.

Here are two recent examples of changes in service:

- BookSurge just launched "Total Design Freedom" where a design team creates a custom book exactly to your vision.

- iUniverse's supported self-publishing offers special programs for books that reach various sales levels, increasing exposure at their alliance partner Barnes & Noble, and can bring out-of-print books back to life.

Comparisons are difficult because the firms offer various packages, and some services require additional charges. Check contract details carefully. Make certain you understand the critical components of rates, rights, and royalties. Then check for any added costs to produce your cover, number of corrections included in price, whether they offer manuscript editing or just spell-check,

and whether editing is mandatory. Don't
assume an item that goes unmentioned
is favorable. As the saying goes: "If it isn't
in your contract, it isn't in your contract."

What You'll Pay for POD

Basic packages have one price, such as
$350 to $600 for all production work,
printing costs, distribution, ISBN, and
listing your book on Amazon, BN.com,
Powell's, Books-A-Million, Waldenbooks,
etc. Your book will also be listed in the
Ingram database for bookstore orders,
and Baker & Taylor for library orders.

The price also covers making your book
available through the POD firm's website
and fulfilling orders placed through the
publisher rather than online booksellers.
You earn higher royalties on those direct
sales than sales discounted for online
booksellers. Most online retailers, like
bookstores want a substantial discount.
Some POD contracts allow you to set the
discount.

The best POD firm will offer you 50 percent discount on books you purchase for
resale, and also 50 percent on any orders

taken and fulfilled through their website. Be aware that a few POD firms don't offer this important online sales channel.

If your production cost is $400 in total, and your book sells at $20, with you earning 50 percent, you earn $10 per book, making back your cost in the first 40 books sold. Once you recoup that cost, you continue to earn 50 percent royalties on all future sales, at no additional cost. Remember, this royalty percentage varies depending on the firm you work with. Check contracts carefully for each publisher you're considering.

We'll discuss web visibility and promotion in Chapter 8 but an important selection criteria is whether your POD firm offers an author page on their website for online orders. If not, you'll have to send readers to the major online retailers, where you receive lower royalties per book than you get from direct POD orders.

Contract Issues

Check POD contracts before choosing a publisher. You may be surprised at how much they vary. Note: These examples are taken from various publishing contracts and not intended to show prefer-ence for one over the other.

Example 1: What you'd like to see:

"AUTHOR grants to the PUBLISHER the non-exclusive, worldwide license to pub-lish the WORK in print, in the English language. The AUTHOR also grants to the PUBLISHER the right to make the work viewable on the PUBLISHER'S web-site, or partner websites, that have en-tered into agreement with the PUBLISHER, in order to facilitate sales of the WORK."

Not this:

"The author grants the non-exclusive right to sell the Work in digital format, including, but not limited to: computer disk, data bases, CD ROM, and any and all other computer and computer related or digital based storage medium, <u>known and unknown</u>."

Example 2: What you'd like to see:

"If you catch errors after the book has been designed, we will correct up to 15 errors for free. For over 15 corrections, you will be charged $50 per hour for the design time required, with a minimum of one hour."

Not this:

"If errors are discovered later that were in the final version approved by the Au-

thor, the Author agrees to pay a new set-up fee of $199.00 to have the errors corrected."

Example 3: What you'd like to see:

"AUTHOR has the right at any time to cancel this agreement within thirty (30) days advance written notice to the PUBLISHER. If the AUTHOR chooses to cancel, all rights to the WORK will revert to the AUTHOR at the end of the thirty (30) day period."

Not this:

"Upon giving thirty (30) days advance notice, the PUBLISHER may terminate publication of the WORK without cause, at which point the rights to the WORK immediately revert to the AUTHOR, subject to any subsidiary rights granted to third parties and to PUBLISHER'S right to sell off any inventory for a period of one (1) year thereafter."

Comparing publishers is not easy, because, like cell phone contracts, they don't make it easy. So narrow the field to those firms who are responsive to your inquiries, who publish books that look professional and then dig in to sort out the parameters that are important to you.

Since we know traditional publishers offer royalties from 2.5 percent to about 12 percent, and the average royalty is 10.7 percent of net, POD books offer an attractive return. POD royalties range from 20 percent to 50 percent, and ebooks generate a higher return due to low production costs. (We'll cover Ebooks in Chapter 4).

Most retail bookstore chains don't order self-published books because there are no co-op advertising fees, no marketing support to create customer demand, and return of unsold copies is not permitted, unless you pay an upfront fee for return service. But it's also true that they don't carry most books, period. They focus on bestsellers that are highly marketed by authors and publishers to spur sales. If your friends ask for your book, a store will readily order it, sometimes acquiring a few copies to keep on hand.

Every good POD firm makes your book available to Ingram for bookstore orders and to Baker & Taylor for public library orders. Libraries generally order a book if patrons request it, so don't assume you can't get your book into libraries. As a start, donate a copy of your book to a library in your town.

If you do a book-signing at a retail store, they may order your book, and will expect a discount, perhaps 20 to 45 percent. If you speak at a library, they generally let you sell the book yourself, and you keep all profits. Donating a percentage of sales is a meaningful gesture. Consider it when you have a great event, and even mention that a percentage of sales goes back to the organization.

Sales Rank Obsession

Writers have a compulsion to check their sales rank at Amazon, but those sales numbers are not as revealing as they seem. It doesn't reflect sales directly through your POD firm. In fact, it doesn't reflect actual sales, but rather the relative position of one book compared to all others sold through Amazon that day.

Librarians and bookseller pay for access to Nielsen BookScan's retail monitoring service. If you must check, at least use salesrankexpress.com, charteo.us, or titlez.com, where you can track current and historic Amazon ranking, and create a chart to monitor sales of all your books. The better barometer, of course, is a royalty check.

Chapter 4

Ebooks

My business is fairly paperless so it's no surprise I've been a proponent of ebooks for a few years. They haven't caught on in the mass market, but there is an audience who loves the immediacy and low cost. Sony and Microsoft make specific handheld ebook reading devices, but most ebooks are read on a Palm device or computer. Most are displayed in a required viewer or as .PDF files, to view in Adobe Acrobat Reader, formatted exactly like a printed book.

Adobe PDF's can be rotated and resized to fit laptop and tablet PC screens. They can be read on Palm handheld devices, and have features to annotate, bookmark, highlight, and even read text aloud.

When you have a final formatted manuscript, you essentially have an ebook. You open your word processing file and save your manuscript as a .pdf (portable document format), using Adobe Acrobat, Macromedia Flash Paper or another utility. The PDF becomes a small file that can be opened by anyone with the free Adobe Reader, yet the purchaser can't alter your text or suddenly claim to be the author.

Your POD contract may offer an ebook version, included in the price or for a small fee. It won't usually make you rich, but it is another viable sales outlet. People are getting used to the immediacy of downloading a book and reading it instantly.

While ebook sales aren't soaring as a replacement for print books, there is one market segment, recently reported by Forbes that experiences enormous growth. The ebook category for Harlequin romance novels is growing at double-digit rates. Apparently romance readers like the instant delivery, anonymous purchases, and ability to carry and read the novels anywhere.

Ebooks are an attractive publishing model because the cost of publishing vanishes and profit margins are high. Avoid signing a book contract that grants exclusive electronic rights to the publisher. You want to retain those rights so you can distribute ebooks on your own.

You can sell ebooks through hundreds of online channels, keeping about 80 percent on each sale, or 100 percent when you sell them on your own. See the Appendix for a few ebook sales channels, and do research to identify your specific niche.

One trend I've noticed recently is price-creep on ebooks. They were originally sold at least 50 percent below list price of a softcover book. Lately I'm seeing too many ebooks priced at $19.99 or $24.95. We all know the cost incurred in writing, but there's almost no cost in producing ebooks. Ebooks priced like print books are over-priced and are hurting the fledgling ebook industry.

Author M.J. Rose has the distinction of writing the first ebook and first self-published novel *Lip Service* chosen by Literary Guild/Doubleday book club.

Advantages of ebooks:

Color images at no printing cost.

Upload to Lulu or Café Press and sell instantly.

Excellent for demonstrating "how-to" techniques and photos.

Hyperlink to an active Table of Contents.

Update and revise your book whenever you wish.

Produce a special edition, such as a large-type version or commemorative cover.

Modify and re-slant an ebook at no cost. Many authors write one book and sell sections as separate ebooks, even customizing them for particular markets, such as:

The Stay-at-Home Parents Guide to _____
The Frequent Fliers Guide to _____
The City Dwellers Guide to _____

Now that you've reviewed your options in self-publishing and POD, and you know you *can* get your book published, let's review productive strategies and technology to aid in manuscript development.

Part 2

You, The Word Processor

■ · ■ · ■ · ■ · ■ · ■ · ■ · ■ · ■ · ■

Chapter 5

The Time to Write

Aah, the romance of being a writer: images of a cabin in the woods, an ocean-front beach house. Funny, we rarely conjure up the reality of writing in sweatpants or on an unmade bed. The allure of "being a writer" has the illusive feeling of solitary contemplation. But it takes work, and plenty of it.

Writing is a process, and revision is a big part of the final product. That's not to say you can't enjoy yourself and indulge a little to make writing a pleasant experience. Packing up your laptop and heading to a café with a fireplace or to a companionable university library is reward for your solitary journey to book completion, so indulge a little. And although writing has a reputation of being a lonely, difficult process, most writers enjoy their work, or they wouldn't do it.

We often think we don't have time to write, but more likely we don't want to start because we'll be interrupted, or don't know where to start. As with any large task, think of one small thing you can do to get moving, and start there.

Whatever it takes to get your wheels turning, surrender yourself to it every day, to strengthen the habit, build critical mass, and keep moving toward your goal.

In *Pen On Fire,* Barbara DeMarco-Barrett shares some hilarious efforts to write a little bit every day, even if it's on a paper bag found in the trunk of her car. The time to write is always now.

Writing Goals
I don't address fear, loathing and the basket of angst often associated with the writing life. I don't believe in writer's block or fear of rejection. It's writing—rearranging the alphabet. It's not hard work; it's your book. If you have anxieties about writing, take Helen Keller's advice: "Feel the fear and do it anyway."

Determine manageable goals to keep your writing on track. Saying: "I want to take a vacation" won't get you very far. So too with saying you want to write a book, finish your book, or get a book published. It won't happen by itself.

Make specific goals and a timeline. Fine-tune them over and over, such as:

1. Research history angle for Chapter 4
2. Submit book proposal to an agent
3. Create marketing plan for first three months
4. Write a first draft of Chapter 5 this month.
5. Write now.

How well do you manage your goals as a writer? Successful people chart their objectives. Strive for working on your top three goals every day. You will get sidetracked. It happens to all of us. When things don't go as planned, see if you can shortcut one of your goals to at least move it ahead a little. Re-evaluate your top three goals every day.

If you tell a child to clean his room, you might wait forever because the instruction is too vague. Instead if you say: Pick up your toys so we can watch a movie," you're more likely to get results.

The same thing happens if you say, "I should write today." Not too specific, is it? Break big writing tasks into smaller jobs and pick one to accomplish within a specific timeframe.

Are you a fan of David Allen? He's a great list-maker and author of *Getting Things Done: The Art of Stress-free Productivity,* (www.davidco.com).

We've only recently become a society that habitually does too many things at once. Allen's productivity strategies can help you stop multi-tasking and learn how to focus again. The core message of *Getting Things Done* is two-fold:

1. Only work on *one thing at a time*, and
2. Everything current gets emptied and re-evaluated daily.

And that means email too.

Production and Revisions
There isn't one right way to sit down and write a book, but good organizational skills will help you stay on track. Most non-fiction authors begin with an outline and first write the parts that come easily, then circle back to more challenging sections. Fiction writers often dive right in but may not really write the first chapter until they finish the book. That's right, we often hear fiction writers say they had

no idea how their book was going to turn out until they got to the end.

And that's all the more reason to avoid laboring over a first draft of material that may or may not stay in the book.

In *Bird by Bird*, which seems to make the top ten list for every writer's favorite books, Anne Lamott stresses the importance of giving yourself permission to write bad first drafts. No one can be expected to compose polished, final prose on the first try. Although it's hard to imagine Shakespeare, Charles Dickens and James Joyce doing manual re-writing, they've all been through enormous effort at re-writing to get from first to last draft.

Give ideas time to take shape. If you get stuck, use freewriting exercises or write in your journal about your book's core message, or a character's motivation. Words and concepts may not all come to you at once, so take time to play with words and see what develops.

Especially when writing fiction, let technology free you. Quickly move through your text using "Edit/Find" to locate that old dog, Buzz, and change his name to Rudy by clicking "Replace all." Use the same trick to move everyone from Georgia to Colorado if the action needs to change to winter.

Once you've devised a workable structure for your book, enjoy the process of writing. It will be with you for a long time. How long? A year is not unusual for a straightforward book that doesn't require a lot of research or interviews. Most books take 3 to 4 years to complete, and many novelists work long years to get a manuscript in perfect shape before submitting to an agent or editor. Set reasonable expectations for yourself, and keep the project from slipping off your radar screen by targeting measurable tasks. Spend some amount of time on the book each day and schedule a few marathon days or evenings each month for solid writing time.

The specific tasks along the way largely depend on the structure of your book. For some books you might need to travel for research, and find you'll be itching to get back to the writing. For another, time needed for interviews and writing up case studies might be exhausting. You reach a plateau where you feel you'll never be finished. That's a good time to review your overall goals, and make sure you're still on track. If your goals are realistic and you break them down to feasible actions, you will make progress, and will get results. If you get stuck, pick something easy you can accomplish to get back on track. Refine a prior chapter and send it to a colleague for critique. Take a break while waiting for a response. Reorganize your outline, do some research, interview a few experts, or read works in your field to re-ignite your energy.

The Last 100 Hours

When you finally have the text nailed down, and your chapters flow, it still takes about 100 hours for reader feedback, final review and editing, reading cover-to-cover, chasing down citations, and submitting for publication. Even writers with a traditional publisher need that huge time push at the end.

Don't get scared though. It's not 100 hours without sleep, just two to three weeks where you won't watch TV, open the mail or read the newspaper. You will use all your available time for the final push to publication, because you're so close to being finished, and it feels so good.

Maybe you're tired of revising, or up against your deadline. This is not the time to rush. Your book has taken shape from a dream to a reality, but the professional editing, formatting and last minute clean up should not be rushed. Even when you think you're done, print the manuscript, put it in a binder, and read it cover-to-cover, or read it aloud. If you love it, and you know your target audience, your readers will love the book too.

When to Stop Writing
The writing process often ignites multiple ideas and paths that may not all fit into one book. Always keep your audience in mind and stay true to your book's core message. Use freewriting exercises to brainstorm when you get stuck or seek a new direction but capture those fragments and save them. When you finish your book, you can organize those ideas for another book or for magazine articles.

Do your best, and revise to improve your work, but at some point you have to stop writing, stop adding more. Let your outline or table of contents (TOC) help you decide how well the text flows. The TOC is particularly handy when you are polishing drafts because it shows how large each chapter is. Eventually you have to stop. A viewer on Rachael Ray's cooking show asked how to peel an onion. Rachael said, "What do you mean? You peel the skin." "Yes, but how do I know when I'm done? When I peel off layer after layer, I only have half an onion left." So, with onions and with writing, you've got to stop when you're done.

Chapter 6

The Writer's Toolbox

At a writing conference recently, a speaker mentioned his methods of finding ideas and staying organized, mostly by clipping articles of interest and sorting them by subject into file folders. An audience member asked the man about his filing system. She asked him three times. It's as though she thought: "If I only knew how to file and retrieve ideas like he does, I could be a better writer."

There is no magic to an organization system, but what works for other people may not suit you. The best system is the file and retrieval technique used by the brain, but computers can't quite match that power. If you use some sort of paper or computer system, you'll be more efficient and in control of all the reference material you need as a writer.

As a computer consultant, I naturally lean toward technology. I feel the more information you store in the computer the easier it is to manage. Everything is in one place and can be retrieved by date, subject, or even keyword. To me, paper files cause many hours of wasted time—moving them, re-piling stacks and heaps, and searching to find a document or fragment from among hundreds of files.

A computer's file structure does a good job of emulating paper folders, yet files seem to grow like mismatched socks in the sock drawer. PCs and Macs have powerful tools to locate and manage files, but if you don't know to look for it, you'd seldom just stumble across it and figure it out. Here's an example, using Windows XP.

Windows Explorer in Windows XP is actually a database, with powerful features and several ways of managing files. You can open Windows Explorer with a right-click on Start and choose Explore, or find it in the Program menu. Right-click on "Explore" to send a shortcut to your desktop. A keyboard shortcut method is to press the keyboard's Window button and press the letter E.

In Vista, look for Vista Explorer. It takes a while to get used to, but you'll see some improvements over Windows Explorer. With Vista Explorer you can easily find documents, pictures, or search for recently changed files. Viewing files in transparent windows makes it even easier to find what you're looking for. The same keyboard shortcut works here: Window button + E.

With both programs, use the Search icon to find files by date and time, by name fragment, or file type. Vista aids your search for pictures by including not just file type, such as .jpg, but camera model as well, assuming your family has more than one digital camera. Vista also allows you to add a keyword to a file, called metadata, to aid in retrieval. If you tag all documents with the metatag "genetics," you can search for all files regardless of type or name, using that metadata tag.

Get Organized
Managing information is easier when a tool works the way you do. Here's a roundup of a few good organizing tools especially valued by writers. Commonly called a "PIM," these are personal information managers. Most of these programs are small enough to run on a portable USB thumb drive, so your data is always with you. If you yearn for good organization, you won't go wrong with any one of these tools. A good organizer

is the single most important tech tool for busy people.

Evernote free version or $49.95	www.evernote.com File and access notes, web-page excerpts, emails, phone messages, addresses, passwords, brainstorms, sketches, documents and more.
InfoSelect free trial then $49.95/yr	www.miclog.com Manage all your random bits of information with three easy commands: Create Note, Create Topic, and Search.
Jotplus free trial then $29.95	www.kingstairs.com/jot My personal favorite. A free-form note application with no specific fields, no fixed structure. Organize your data any way you wish. Re-organize with drag-and-drop ease or click to sort. Each note can hold up to a million characters, large enough for the entire text of *Pride and Prejudice* or *Oliver Twist*. A single Jot+ Notes document can store everything you need for book projects, with rich formatting, embedded images and more.
OneNote free trial then retail near $99	www.office.microsoft.com/en-us/onenote If you don't know the simplicity of the other offerings here,

	you might love Microsoft OneNote. A little bloated, but very flexible. It's a digital notebook to gather text, photos, audio, video, even handwriting all in one place. Emphasis is on sharing with colleagues.
Treepad free version or $29.95	www.treepad.com Get a grip on data, notes, bills, projects, clients, addresses, letters, speeches, research, collections, web pages, links, bibliographic listings. Offers a special fiction-writers template.

Larger programs, such as Act! and Outlook, do more for you, by combining email with contact information, task lists and calendar, at www.act.com, www.microsoft.com/outlook.

Maybe these tools aren't the ultimate idea of fun for you, but there is a huge cost to being disorganized. Choose a tool and give yourself a few weeks to apply its principles. You'll find it much easier to stay on task.

If you're an Outlook Express user, I have bad news. Microsoft abandoned Outlook Express on Vista computers, replacing it

with Windows Mail, which does not inter-
face with Windows Calendar.

The Right Tool for the Job

A writer's best tools may include a
leather-bound journal and a favorite
Mont Blanc pen, but are more likely to be
a pile of electronic gadgets that require
maintenance and good karma to keep
them working. Unless you're a gadget
freak, every tech purchase is a pain in
the bank account.

And, some writers don't like change. You
might be reluctant to upgrade your computers, but if you wait too long, it's more
difficult to make the move. If you think
only of the cost, you'll overlook the productivity edge you'll get with better technology. If your equipment doesn't fit your
style, don't hate it—replace it.

Dispose of computer equipment carefully,
according to local environmental regula-
tions and ensure your data is erased or
the disk is formatted to wipe the contents
of your files before you discard it. Search
online for free software utilities to com-
pletely wipe data from a disk.

If you carry a Palm or handheld device with keyboard, you will be ready to write whenever inspiration strikes. Once the ideas start flowing, tune out other distractions, such as telephone and email until you get your thoughts down. Anne Lamott speaks of always having paper and a pen in her back pocket.

I'm not artistic but I've had "painter's envy" for many years. The little wooden boxes, lovely colors stained on well-worn rags, are evidence of an artist at work. A painter's tools always look like they're on the way to being something else. As writers, we have more tools and tech tricks in our word processing suite than Hemingway could have dreamed of when he toted his Underwood typewriter to Africa and Cuba. Yet, our writing doesn't start to look like a book right from page one.

Among the tools available to help turn out great writing, the best resource is a word processing program, such as Word, Word Perfect or Star Office. In addition to writing on the computer, you can create outlines, character sketches, and organize yourself with timelines, templates, and research notes. If you're already a tech whiz, you'll still find a few tips here to speed up your time at the keyboard.

You may remember what writing a book was like before computers, but it's hard to imagine being as productive without them. Would you want to go back to the rewrite process using a typewriter or pen? In return for the speed and convenience of using computers for word processing and organizing our books, the tradeoff is ownership of more technology than we care to manage.

As a tech consultant, here are the top six issues writers ask me. If you have other issues not addressed here, email me at Helen@cclarity.com or post questions at the Q & A forum at www.cclarity.com.

1. Backup Guilt

Techies prophesize that there are two kinds of people in the world: Those who have lost all their data, and those who will. So, back it up or risk having to start over. Backup devices range from disk, tape, USB, and CD to external hard drives and remote solutions. What's best for you? Whatever method you'll use regularly. It can be as simple as drag & drop from your desktop to a USB drive, or a remote system that backs up your data while you're sleeping. I usually caution that a backup next to your computer isn't really a backup. If your office sustains water damage or theft, offsite or remote backup is a safer choice. Genie-Soft.com and Mozy.com are two popular secure, online backup services.

2. Laptop or Desktop

People resist being tethered to a desk when they can work wirelessly anywhere. Today's lightweight laptop and notebook (under four pound) computers offer great screens, large capacity storage and long battery life. As the computer becomes a bigger part of your life, why not work where you want? At the office, meetings, home, car, hotel, plane, airport, café, or your mother-in-law's kitchen table.

If you work on both a laptop and desktop, keep in mind it's never easier to have data in two places instead of one. You need discipline to keep your work organized. Good products that synchronize your work between two computers include BeInSync, Laplink and PCAnywhere.

> ### Get peak performance from a laptop battery
>
> When the words are flowing, you don't want to look at your power meter and find your battery is running low. Here's how to get more power.
>
> Rechargeable laptop batteries last for about 300-500 charge/discharge cycles, which equates to about 12 to 18 months of regular use. They need to be run down and recharged often, to recognize what a full charge is. When running on battery, use of peripherals, such as wi-fi adapters, printers and multimedia programs drain the battery faster than routine file usage. If you need to get an extra 30 minutes of battery time, close unused programs, turn off wi-fi, and dim the screen.

3. Email Overload

Are you chained to your email? The invention of email as a communication tool doesn't require we respond to every message with immediacy.

When you look at your Inbox, handle any messages you can deal with quickly to keep them from piling up. Consider limiting your email activity to three times a day to avoid the frequent distraction. Clutter experts recommend handling things only once—whether its bills, kitchen chores or closet clutter. Same with email: Delete it, act on it, or put it away.

Email Tips:

- Use filters to put messages into folders by topic so you can find them easily, and delete read messages daily.

- Hold Shift while deleting messages and bypass the trash entirely.

- Look in your Sent folder and delete messages older than 30 or 60 days. When you finish a large project, back up your email folder and then purge old messages from your current email folders.

- Did you know you can email a file directly from within Microsoft Office? Click "File/Send to:> mail recipient" and it will open in your email program, attached and ready to send, as soon as you insert the recipient's email address. For web mail and AOL users, it's not quite so easy, as this technique works only in POP (post-office protocol) email programs that use a mail reader such as Netscape, Outlook, Outlook Express, SeaMonkey or Thunderbird, rather than web mail.

Watching Your Time Go Down the Drain
Email has become important in our lives, yet we receive little training in this important communication tool. Email just floats out there saying "Can't you control me?"

Controlling email is easy if you learn to manage your time wisely, pay attention to grammar and etiquette, and gain basic proficiency to find, file and follow-up on your communications. But is your email managing you? Procrastinators pay a price for "I'll do it later" tendencies, when hundreds of messages pile up in the In-box, needing to be re-read over and over before deciding whether to delete or keep them. And keeping them just makes more clutter—more places to look for wayward correspondence.

Why do we read email all day long? Because we can. It doesn't mean it is efficient or a good use of your time. Would you run to the mailbox every half-hour to see if the mail carrier has added anything?

When email was a novelty and a secret pleasure of the techno-savvy, we all used to check it a couple times a day, through a dial-up connection, and stare in amazement that someone sent us a message from near or far. Now, with always-on, high-speed Internet connections, we've fallen into the habit of checking email too often. The instant connectivity becomes a constant interruption, draining our concentration.

The witty David Bouchier, essayist and author of *Writer at Work*, says "Computers made writing easier, and then email made it almost impossible."

If email overload is a problem for you, experiment with ways to control it. Try to check email just at specific times of day, or limit yourself to three sessions. See if you can spend a solid 15 minutes reading messages and replying, instead of numerous interruptions throughout the day. Then close the program or at least turn off the sound notification symbol, so you aren't aware every moment a message arrives. It isn't the interruption so much as our inability to estimate how much time things take in the online world. A simple request from someone can send you clicking away on an unplanned 30-minute research project.

Another way to stop the flow of unnecessary email is to use what I call DNR. With no disrespect to those who recognize DNR as the acronym for "do not resuscitate," we need it to end the endless ping-pong of email messages. So I've modified DNR to mean, "do not reply." Include it or a comment such as "No reply needed" (NRN) to put an end to "thank you for the thank you" messages.

Email Etiquette

- You're a writer, so spelling, grammar, and punctuation really matter. Don't get sloppy with email just because it's quick.

- Remember to address multiple recipients as a blind carbon copy (BCC) to avoid giving away your email address list.

- Always proof the subject line since spell-check doesn't.

- Don't hit "Send" too fast. One way to avoid accidentally sending a message before you're ready is to fill in the recipient's address <u>after</u> you compose, add any attachments, and proof the message.

Back Up Your Email

Do you know how to back up your email? Users of web-based mail services don't have this worry but those of us who store email on our computers need a backup now and then. There is always a risk of your mailbox becoming corrupt or damaged.

You can back up your email by finding the export option in your mail program, or searching for a "Mail" or an "Inbox" folder, and copying the entire folder. If you're not sure where to find the mail folder, use Windows Explorer. Search for files modified with the current date and your Inbox will be one of those files.

Email is very bulky, with Inbox, Sent, Trash and other folders consuming huge amounts of disk space. Backing up to another computer or to a portable USB drive is a quick solution. Knowing you have a backup as an archive, you'll be less reluctant to purge a few hundred messages from your "Sent" folder.

Cut Down on Spam

Spam is a terrible drain on our personal productivity, and creates doubt about the safety of messages. If you respond to spam, you're inadvertently verifying your address and inviting more.

The Federal Trade Commission is holding a "Spam Summit" this year, to further address the problem of fraudulent, deceptive and offensive email.

Here are five things you can do today to cut down on spam:

1. Use a second, free email account, like a yahoo.com address, when you have to provide an email address online, never giving out your real address.

2. Adjust your browser to prevent running scripts imbedded in programs without your knowledge. Look under "Tools/Options" or "Edit/Preferences" for this setting.

3. Use your Internet provider's spam blocker. Check their website if you need help.

4. Keep anti-virus and anti-spyware software running, and check them frequently. Most now include spam filters, automatically blocking sus-

picious messages. See CNET.com for updated information on vendors offering software suites to protect your computer from intrusion.

5. Make rapid use of the Delete button. In fact, press Shift + Delete and you'll bypass the trash, sending the messages away forever.

4. Research Tools

How did we ever do effective research BC (before computers)? While we relied on librarians, even their resources were limited to outdated documents, making it difficult to cross-reference or find specific resources.

Writers often ask for help tracking all the research involved in large projects. Here are three strategies:

1. Save all files and folders on your computer. This is an essential step. Include email messages and web pages, as well as documents you generate.

2. Scan paper files so everything is in the project folder in the computer.

3. Use a web page that links to all your sources or online bookmark site, such as del.icio.us, digg or furl.

Web tools like Wikipedia and some of the new generation websites, known as "Web 2.0," are social networking sites with content contributed by anyone with computer access.

Consider the source when conducting any online research, verify facts, dates and credentials before using material found online. We're conditioned to finding good information online, but "factual" entries at social networking sites, including Wikipedia and Digg, can be very superficial.

See Effective Web Searching in Chapter 8 for some fresh ideas and best tools for searching online, beyond Google.

5. Slow Computer

If your computer is not performing well, or is slowing you down, read "Before You Call Tech Support," a free article posted at www.cclarity.com/techsupport.htm for advice on protecting your data and your nerves, before undertaking a repair project. Forget the days when computers were a huge investment. Today's computers offer great power at low prices, and most heavy users upgrade about every two years. If you wait too long to upgrade, you'll likely find much of your old software and hardware won't work with a new computer, making migration a costly project.

6. Wasting Time

Use technology to your advantage. Think of tech time as your most productive hours and stay focused. When your mind wanders, pop ideas into a to-do list. Gotta send an email? Compose a draft and save it for later. Then, send all your outgoing mail at once. Close your email to minimize distraction and deal with the responses later. Email is a huge time sink, and it requires discipline to use it as a communication tool, not a popularity contest.

When we start and stop our work too often, we give up the sense of process and the satisfaction of completion. Think of it as your bill-paying process: If you still pay bills by hand, you need the bills, checkbook, calculator, pen and stamps all in one place. Do the same with your writing. Have all the ideas, tools, notes and goals in place when you sit down and keep at it until you're done.

Another way writers lose focus is by talking more than actually writing. Most writers are social beings in a solitary job, and share a certain pleasure in the camaraderie of other writers.

The support of colleagues is invaluable, but we need to avoid spending so much time talking about writing that we don't actually get much writing done. Writing generally means hours and hours spent alone, week after week. If you have a deadline, you need to protect your time and make yourself accountable so you stay on track, so your writing can flow.

Alice Flaherty, author of *The Midnight Disease: The Drive to Write, Writer's Block and the Creative Mind*, knows what it means to grasp an idea when the muse strikes. "I strain my nerves for the faintest sense of the feeling that I should write, the feeling that my feet are starting to lift off the ground. Although I sit down to write every day at five in the morning, on the days when my muse has left me, I can no longer pretend that I sit down because I am in control of the situation. I am not writing but doing penance for all the days when the muse spoke and I failed to listen."

Chapter 7

Computer Power Tools

Word Processing Power
Getting around in your manuscript is fast and efficient if you have some fluency with word processing. Well, okay, maybe it's more like tedious and efficient. Basic computer skills and the ability to follow instructions are all you need. Even if you still love to write longhand, at some point, putting your book into the computer lets you see the manuscript, as it's taking shape. You can revise chapter by chapter, do global formatting and replace text throughout, as you polish your book. Most word processing programs have the same commands and features. This section refers to Microsoft Word, the most common choice, and offers a review of many productive tools for working on your book.

Turn Clutter into Piles of Success
For many writers, the volume of information needed for research seems to grow with each new project. And some writers

work best amid piles of words. I have a few clients in the PhD category: "piled high and deep."

Whatever your style, if you spend too much time moving stacks and looking for documents, you've got clutter. Consider a master reference document in Word or Excel to help you track documents, sources, and keep a list of web links for everything you researched and cited. You have to keep a reference trail anyway, and pasting references into a computer document is more efficient than creating clutter by printing everything you come across.

You can create a table of contents to keep track of your own note files, even as they grow to 40 or 50 pages. Highlight text and change its format from "Normal" to a "Heading 1," or "Heading 2" and follow the steps shown below to create a table of contents. It's so much faster than hunting through paper.

If you need to keep source material, be diligent about a good computer filing system so the documents are all in one searchable place. Use your scanner for digital images of articles and clippings and store them where you can find them: in the computer instead of a closet.

Scanning software turns paper documents into image files. If you scan and use optical character recognition, (OCR), the scanned document can still be read as text, rather than an image. You can edit the text file in your word processor, usually with about 80 to 90 percent accuracy.

Copyright Usage

Respect copyright on everything you quote or include in your work. That goes for images and cartoons as well as text. Even if you own Microsoft Office, you don't have rights to use its clipart for profit. If you read the clipart collection license information, it states it is for personal use, not profit. I'll spare you all the legalese with this excerpt: "You may copy and use these images, clip art, animations, sounds, music, shapes, video clips, and templates identified for such use in documents and projects that you create. You may distribute those documents and projects non-commercially. If you wish to use these media elements or templates for any other purpose, go to www.microsoft.com/permission to learn whether that use is allowed."

There it states: "You may not use clipart to advertise your business. You may not use clipart to illustrate the chapters of a book."

Even if you purchase a license to use copyrighted art, the license often limits print and electronic reproduction rights to a specific number of uses, which prohibits reproducing images in a book or on a website. If you don't know a graphic designer, you can search online for royalty-free images and pay a one-time license fee for art to illustrate your projects.

Capture and Edit Web Copy and Screenshots
While respecting copyright ownership, it's sometimes useful to grab information or screenshots from web pages as documentation. If you don't have the option to right-click to save an image, here's how to capture a segment of a page.

1. Press PrtScr [print-screen] to copy the image to the Clipboard.

2. Open the Paint program (click Start/Programs/Accessories/Paint.) Once there, click "Edit/Paste" and the web page will appear as an image.

3. Move the mouse to the upper left corner and you'll see a bold black four-point arrow. Use that arrow to move the page a bit to the right so you can get to the cropping tool, which looks like cross-hairs. Place that cropping tool where you want it to cut away what you don't need. When you have exactly what you want, you can copy the image into other documents.

4. Click "File/Save as" and save as a .jpg, .gif or .bmp, the three most common image file types. Note where you are saving it, such as My Pictures, or your book's project folder.

If this seems like too much work, you can download SnagIt or a PrintScreen program from download.com. Remember, screenshots may be useful for your reference or background information, but avoid using the material in a way that infringes on copyrights. I'm using clipped screenshots below, to illustrate parts of program screens.

Multitasking: A Writer's Best Friend
Windows is plural. Learn to use two or more programs at once. Each open program uses only a small portion of your

processor's capacity. You can work in several programs at once, switching among them, or re-size documents to see them side-by-side. This is a neat trick when editing and revising, or doing online research and viewing your manuscript simultaneously.

The controls shown below illustrate how to move and resize screens. Grab an edge and re-size it to fit on half the screen, so you can see the other window behind it. Double-click anywhere in the blue title bar to restore to full size, and grab a window anywhere in that same title bar to move it where you want.

Table of Contents

For a non-fiction book, you'll generally want a Table of Contents (TOC). The following screen shots show the three-step process to create a TOC in a typical word processing program. Highlight your chapter headings and sub-heads, and change their format from "Normal" to the "Heading" style you desire: Heading 1, 2, 3 for example. Click a blank space at the top of your document, then click "Insert/Index & Tables." Choose "Table of Contents" and it will appear at the top of your manuscript. As you make changes, right-click on the table of contents and choose "Update Entire Table."

96

TOC Example-Release Your Writing - Microsoft Word

File Edit View Insert Format Tools Table FlashPaper Window Help

100% Normal Arial 11 B U

The result ...

Index

While a TOC is found in the front of a book, an index, or concordance, is an alphabetical listing of principal words in a book, not just chapter headings and sub-headings. An index is placed at the back of the book for reference. Word processing programs can assist with what would be a very tedious manual task. Here's how to build an index, using Microsoft Word as an example:

1. Throughout your manuscript, highlight the first usage of text you want Word to search for and mark it as an index entry, as shown below. From the top tool bar click "Insert/Index & Tables" and choose the format you prefer. Make sure to enter the text exactly as it appears in the document.

Tip: A handy keyboard shortcut, if you're dexterous, is to mark an index entry by pressing Alt + Shift + X.

Mark Index Entry ? X

Index
Main entry: |
Subentry: |
Options
⊙ Cross-reference: See
⦿ Current page
○ Page range
Bookmark: ▼
Page number format
☐ Bold
☐ Italic

This dialog box stays open so that you can mark multiple index entries.

Mark | Mark All | Cancel

2. Indicate if the word is a sub-entry of another category, and if you should cross-reference it with another term. For infrequent, but important words, click "Mark All," but for common words like "table" you might prefer to mark each meaningful reference manually.

3. Cross-check your entire index carefully. Click on every link in the final index and be sure it goes to the correct page. You may find an error or two, with unintended reference links. You can manually correct or delete those. To see the results of your Index efforts, right-click on the Index at the back of your book, and click "Update table."

Manuscript Layout

A table of contents also serves as a great outlining tool. Begin making headings, per the above TOC screenshots so you can organize your book. But wait until you're near the end of your final manuscript before creating the index. It requires enough labor that you don't want to have to do it twice.

The index creation process adds paragraph markings throughout your document, and makes it more difficult to proofread.

Here's an example with the Index feature turned on:

¶
Let's·take·a·brief·look·at·traditional·
publishing{·XE·"traditional·publishing"·\t·
"*See*·Publishing"·}·methods,·before·we·
launch·into·publishing·*your*·way.·¶
¶

If you turn off the paragraph marks, you can no longer see which words are indexed. As a result, it's generally among the final production chores. Most non-academic books use a simple indexing format. If you need a more elaborate index, your publisher may have software to create it.

The Mechanics of Writing for Publication
Going from blank page to finished manuscript requires skill with a few document management techniques. There's a real psychological benefit to having your book look like a book right from the beginning. The entire production process requires a large commitment of time, energy and intellectual resources. Envisioning your book as it develops helps fuel the desire to persevere.

Here's a rundown using Microsoft Word as an example. The same techniques apply to formatting self-published books, ebooks, or those submitted to a publisher.

Document formatting can be as simple as deciding spacing and page margins, or as complex as using a template to create a unique font for headings, sub-headings graphics and footnotes.

Manuscript Formatting

You probably already use document-formatting basics, such as spelling and grammar checking, making headers, and inserting footnotes or endnotes for your book.

When writing early drafts of your manuscript, use a special symbol to refer to gaps where you want to return your attention, such as the caret (<<<) or your initials. Later you can search for all occurrences of <<< or your initials, and return to the spots that need your attention, using "Edit/Find."

An important formatting tip is to avoid non-tabs, where you press the spacebar to move where you want text to appear. Those spaces will be lost when you convert the manuscript to the publisher's software. Use the "Tab" key or indent. Also avoid forcing page breaks and section breaks if possible. When you change to the final format for publication, you'll follow the publisher's requirements for margins and page setup, and your page and section breaks will change.

Other than page numbers, hold off on headers, footers, margins and special fonts. All of that is very likely to change, and to change many times over. Depending on your publisher, you may be limited to a few specific highly readable fonts and they will want your document as clean as possible.

You will probably also write your drafts with a normal full size page margin of 8.5" x 11," for convenience in editing and printing numerous drafts. All the formats, line breaks and margins will change when you create your final manuscript in a smaller page size.

Power Tools for Computing
Ready for more? Here are some basic word processing tricks for writers.

Cut & Paste
Writers live by shortcuts such as the toolbar icons to cut, copy and paste. But what do you do on a screen or web page

where there is no editing toolbar? Here are two choices:

1. Highlight the text and right click. If no menu is available, a right-click will usually have the most frequently used commands, including cut and paste.

2. Rely on the old keyboard shortcuts. Press CTRL + X for cut, CTRL + C for copy, and CTRL + V for paste. You can even use this trick to copy and paste from web pages, email, notes, documents, and spreadsheets.

Dictionary & Thesaurus

You can add to Word's built-in dictionary, already containing over 50,000 words, by clicking "Add" while checking spelling. Choose "Ignore" for a one-time oddity like the term: Emblazo, and "Ignore All" when you're writing an article that mentions Samiz Libournagioro a few dozen times. Choose "Add" if Samiz will be in your life forever, so the spell-check program will not flag it as an error in the future.

Banish AutoFormat

Microsoft products, more than any others, are programmed to do certain tasks automatically, sometimes to our amusement and sometimes to great frustration, especially when it takes control over your formats. It's maddening when an underline in Word turns into a whole line you didn't want and can't always delete. Here are two easy remedies. First, hit a space when you've drawn the line as far as you want, and it will break the automatic format. Second, if you notice the line being drawn to the end of your margin, click "Edit/Undo" and it will remove the autoformat.

Control Crazy Formatting

Start a numbered list with a number 1, for example, and it continues to number subsequent paragraphs until you grow old. To stop it, click "Edit/Undo Auto Format" when you no longer want it to repeat numbers.

Do the same to control bullet points. After the last bulleted item, press "Enter" to stop the automatic formatting, or uncheck the bullet icon in the toolbar.

Create PDFs

If you have the full version of Adobe Acrobat or a similar utility you can create PDFs—unalterable versions of any documents: such as articles, excerpts, or sample chapters. When we download tax forms from Internal Revenue, they are PDFs. We can't alter them or type directly on them, and they don't shift around like word processing documents do.

To produce a PDF from your document, if you have the full version of Adobe or another PDF maker, click "File/Print" and choose PDF instead of your usual printer. Name the file and pay attention to where you're saving it.

Edit/Find & Replace

Use a macro, as you'll see below, or click "Edit/Find & Replace" to change "bs" to "business" every time you type it or your custom abbreviations such as changing "corp" to "Inc." Create your personal shorthand with macros for specific industry words or terms specific to your book.

Ergonomics

Proper posture, adaptive tools and dictation software can alleviate strain and prevent Carpal Tunnel Syndrome (CTS). CTS is a repetitive motion injury, not limited to computer users. In many industries, assembly line workers, machine operators and parts handlers are also susceptible to repetitive stress injury. With the prevalence of the computer and the mouse as a pointing device, the incidence of CTS injury has skyrocketed among frequent users.

According to a medical abstract at pcrsonalmd.com, pressure on the median nerve in the wrist can cause pain, numbness and tingling in the hand, wrist or fingers. Check the Appendix for links to more guidance, including stress solutions and ergonomic alternatives to the traditional mouse and keyboard devices.

As one who uses the computer all day, every day, one tip I can offer is to alter your mouse usage. I joke that I've become "ambi-moustrous" because I use the mouse well with either hand. I've trained myself to use the mouse with my left hand at one computer, and use a touchpad mouse on another. The touchpad mouse looks remarkably like a miniature Etch-a-Sketch toy. It stays in one place, does not need a pad underneath, and responds to a touch or sweep of the fingertip for quick movement. Laptop computers and some specialty keyboards have the touchpad built into the keyboard, letting you access the mouse without extensive reaching. A wireless mouse also assures it's within comfortable reach for your arm.

Format Painter
In the standard Word toolbar, there is a small paintbrush icon labeled "Format Painter." If you've never tried it, you're in for some fun. Let's presume your entire manuscript is formatted in Georgia font, 12-point. But you paste in a few paragraphs from an article you once wrote, and it's Arial, 14-point and bold. Click and hold the Format Painter, then brush it across a paragraph that is formatted exactly as you wish: Georgia, 12-point. You're essentially copying the format, not the text. Then, click and drag to paint the brush over the Arial 14 bold paragraph and it will match your Georgia 12-point font perfectly.

FTP: Upload Files to the Web
FTP (file transfer protocol) is a free utility to move files from your computer to the web. It used to be the only easy tool but

there are now many other methods to transfer files. Most web hosts include FTP among their transfer options. FTP is valuable not only for posting text to your site, but photos, clips of your work and PDFs (portable document format). You can get an FTP program by searching for "free FTP" at download.com. It's a handy tool when you want to upload a quick photo or article to your website.

Grammar and Reading Level Statistics

For better grammar and spell-checking, click "Options" in SpellCheck and choose "Show readability statistics" so you get the score or count on spelling and grammar, especially passive sentences. The Flesch Reading Ease score, shown below, is a language tool that measures reading difficulty of text. It does so by determining the complexity of sentence structure, syllables and words per sentence. Most Americans read at the 7th or 8th grade level, and newspapers are commonly written to that level. Use the readability statistics to test your writing level, and to keep an eye on the passive voice we all try to avoid.

Readability Statistics	?	X

Averages

Sentences per Paragraph	1.0
Words per Sentence	25.0
Characters per Word	5.6

Readability

Passive Sentences	0%
Flesch Reading Ease	42.7
Flesch-Kincaid Grade Level	12.0

Graphics

Insert .jpg or .gif images for your book's graphics. Title each image and use a text box (from Word's Drawing toolbar) to indicate title and placement in your manuscript. At the back of your manuscript document, include a list of all graphics by file name, and indicate page number for placement.

Keyboard vs. Mouse

Christopher Sholes invented the keyboard for typewriters in 1868, as a complex array of gears and letters of the alphabet carved into metal sticks designed to roll upward to strike an inked ribbon making an impression on paper. Did you know the keyboard layout of the alphabet was arranged to actually slow down the typing process? Keys jammed if they were too close together because the early mechanisms were imperfect. The QWERTY keyboard is named for the first six letters in the top row of alphabetic keys. We are still living with this basic keyboard Mr. Sholes designed, despite efforts to improve on the layout.

I hate to be the one to tell you this, but the mouse isn't perfect either. In fact, using a mouse can decrease your productivity because it takes so long to align the mouse with the desired target. That's where keyboard shortcuts can really pay off. Download a list of popular keyboard shortcuts at www.releaseyourwriting.com/keyboard.html

Here's how to tame a run-away mouse. To avoid highlighting all over a document when you mean to grab just a bit of text, use the Shift key to anchor the start of your highlighting, and the arrow keys to control the block of text.

Macros to Automate Keystrokes

A macro is an automated series of keystrokes, to create a shortcut, widely used in word processing and spreadsheets. Start at "Tools/Macro" in most word processing programs, and assign a name to the macro, such as your initials. When you activate the macro tool, it records as you type a sequence or formatting. The computer tracks your every move with the mouse or keyboard. When you click Stop, your shortcut is saved. Press Alt + F8 to invoke it any time. Assign a keyboard shortcut such as Ctrl + T for title, and you won't have to continually re-type your long book title.

If you've never done a macro, start with a simple one: Click "Tools/Macro/Record New Macro." Create a name for the macro such as "title." Type your name or your book's name and click "Stop." Then open a document and press Alt + F8. You should see a list of macros including the "title" one you created. Choose "Run" to insert the macro. Macros are written in Visual Basic programming language, not quite as friendly as most software. If you get a scary programming error when you're experimenting, just back out or close the window without saving your changes and try again. Take time to read the Help files in Word or Excel if you want to use them well.

Page Setup

Choose "Custom" to set margins as required by your publisher. Standard page
sizes are 5.5 x 8.25", 6 x 9", etc. This will
depend on the specs from your publisher. Most POD firms offer this information in their online submission package.

Save as Web Page

If you want to post a word processing
document on the web, click "File/Save
as" and choose .html (hypertext markup
language) instead of .doc. You can then
export the file directly to the web, via
FTP. Word processing formats are especially bloated so check your .html pages
before loading to the web. To do so, open
your web browser and click "File/Open,"
pointing to the document you just saved
as .html. You may need to edit out stray
formatting or change a few font sizes to
have it appear correctly online. Check the
page in several browsers to be sure the
format looks right and the images appear.

Saving Files and Drafts

Effective file management includes using
folders to organize parts of your book
project and saving files with logical

names. Avoid long file names so you can readily see names displayed. If each file begins with the same long name, you have to scroll and stretch to see the full names. Try to avoid saving each chapter in a separate file or on a separate disk. That's an anxiety attack waiting to happen. Instead, enjoy seeing your manuscript take shape as a book, using a comprehensive outline or creating a table of contents to keep yourself organized.

Re-save your manuscript frequently, and update the name to reflect your recent changes, such as "draft1", "draft2", "cut Sam", "edited1", and "book indexed." It may sound compulsive but it always allows you to go back to an earlier draft for something you may have cut, with the prior draft names as a guide.

As you revise your manuscript, save prior versions if you can't bear to sacrifice your beautiful prose. The revision process is less stressful if you realize you can always go back. "Re-vision" is a way to improve and tighten your writing, with every draft.

✓ Draft 1 is a breeze: just get the words on the page.

✓ Draft 2 is a fitness test: Does that text belong there? Should I move this passage up a chapter?

✓ Draft 3 is all about research: Do your fact checking, get permissions to quote passages, and make sure all references and sources are 100 percent correct.

✓ Draft 4 leads to more: By now, your book is looking good. It reads well, everything is in the right order, and it's accurate. This is when you're ready to share it with advisors and editors for comments on suggested changes.

Speech Recognition Software

Most writing books overlook the value of speech recognition software as an aid to writing and the revision process.

Formerly known primarily as assistive technology, or access tools for people with cognitive disabilities, these programs have moved into mainstream use today. People who don't like to, or don't want to type, can dictate right into the computer, have the text read back, and even make corrections verbally.

Think about it: Instead of revising your book at your desk, your computer can read the entire manuscript aloud while you're sweating and swaying on the treadmill.

It takes at least 20 minutes to train the software to interpret the nuances of your speech, but the technology has improved tremendously in recent years and benefits are enormous. The most popular text-to-speech software is Dragon NaturallySpeaking. The "text to speech" toolbar in Microsoft Office 2003 reads back any highlighted text aloud. Use the "Speech" icon in the Control Panel to choose the computer-generated voice you prefer and to control reading speed.

Microsoft Vista offers a newer "Windows Speech Recognition" feature to enhance productivity by limiting mouse and keyboard use. It uses a more natural dialog with "say what you see" techniques to open and switch between programs, dictate email, and browse the web by speaking links, or saying the number shown on a page of links.

If you're a frequently confused user of Microsoft's Help menu, you'll get rid of some frustration by saying aloud "How do I change margins?" and have the solution read right back to you.

Learn more and watch a demo at www.microsoft.com/enable/demos/wind owsvista/speech.aspx

Tables

Insert a table with specific rows and columns to keep random text from jumping around. Click "Table" in your word processing toolbar, and specify the number of rows and columns. You can always right-click to add or delete rows. Right-click on a table to add shading and other formatting.

Templates

Instead of starting with a blank document for everything you do, you can create formatted templates ready to use for queries, your resume, or a release form for interviews and reprint permissions. In Word, click "File/New/Template" to create and save a template. To use your new template, click "File/New" instead of "File/Open," because you're making a new document based on that template instead of the default Normal.dot template. To find your templates in the future, instead of starting with "File/Open" in your word processor, choose "File/New" and all your templates will be visible.

If you're new to the business side of writing, the Small Business Administration (www.sba.gov) can help you get started with downloadable templates for everything from a break-even analysis to a start-up expense worksheet at www.score.org/template_gallery.html

Word Count
If you love nothing else about writing by computer, I'm sure you love clicking "Tools/Word count." It's every writer's friend.

From this point on, no matter how many drafts you go through, you're getting closer and closer to the final product. Now, take a look at how a spreadsheet program can keep you on track, and then we'll get serious about marketing your work.

Excel Spreadsheets
Excel spreadsheets are perfect for people who like to track information: passwords, frequent computer commands, interview questions, lists of newspapers and radio stations for promotions. And financial data is what Excel does best. If you're not familiar with Excel, give it a little time, and you will appreciate its organizational structure, compared to the frenetic behavior of text in a word processor. Promoting your book gives you many reasons to use Excel to track your activities, sales and success.

Release Your Writing is about words, of course, not numbers, but here's a quick rundown on some of the useful functions of Excel:

Styles and Colors
The Excel toolbar makes it easy to add borders, colorful shading and gridlines. Make massive charts of goals, plot outlines, income and expenses, marketing budgets, or even graph your monthly sales or your personal fitness routine.

Smarter Cut & Paste

In Excel, you can copy fields and click "Edit/Paste Special" for a variety of choices, including transposing rows and columns, pasting in values rather than formulas, or pasting column widths so the program doesn't change their size.

Formats

Click "Format/Cells" to control the look of currency, dates or special number series. Excel does a good job of predicting what formats you want. Type "Jan Feb Mar" in three cells, or "Mon Tues Weds," or "1 2 3" and highlight those cells. Grab the lower right corner of the highlighted range, and drag the border down or across. Excel will expand the list to complete the series.

Multiple Sheets

Excel worksheets display a tab at the bottom for Sheet 1, Sheet 2, Sheet 3, up to 16 in a standard spreadsheet. Using these sheets, you can keep all related work in a single file. Perhaps Sheet 1 is a long list of marketing projects and ideas for promoting your work, Sheet 2 is your mailing list, ready for a mail merge, and Sheet 3 is where you track your business expenses. Right-click on the sheet tabs to rename or move them. Click "Insert/Worksheet" when you're ready to add another sheet.

			Insert...
			Delete
			Rename
			Move or Copy...
			Select All Sheets
			View Code

/ Mailing List \ **Expenses** /

Another benefit of listing activities in Excel is that you can track what works and what doesn't. For example, if you record $75 spent on an ad, follow up by noting any spike in book sales or the number of inquires resulting from the ad.

Excel Formulas
Equations are easy in Excel with simple math symbols. You've probably noticed all rows are numbered and columns are coded with letters in Excel. That's the trick to performing actions, such as formulas and formatting. You perform actions based on specific cell addresses such as A1+B1.

Basic math symbols are: add (+), sub-tract (-), multiply (*), and divide (/). You already know what the equal sign (=) does. Formulas are written in parenthe-ses, such as =sum(a1:b7) to add up the numbers in a range of rows or columns.

If you want numbers to act as text, insert an apostrophe before the numbers and Excel will ignore their math value. (Ex: for a list of ISBNs, use '1589398157 to avoid formatting as a number, with commas.

Expense and Revenue Tracking
Looking at the chart below, if you want to sum the numbers in column C, you would type this formula in cell C7: =sum(C2:C6) to get the total of $656.

	A	B	C
1	Date	Expense	Amount
2	7/15/2007	post card mailing	42
3	8/1/2007	writing group membership	75
4	8/5/2007	book production fees	400
5	10/15/2007	shipping review copies	14
6	11/10/2007	holiday ad	125
7			$656

By using formulas, if your writing group membership expense grows from $75 to $150, the total will change automatically, because it is the sum of whatever is in the five rows above it.

You can use the same Excel spreadsheet to track sales. To calculate your sales tax liability, assuming a 3 percent state sales tax, type this formula in cell D8: =D7*.03

	A	B	C	D	E
1	**Sales**	**Copies**	**Price**	**Total**	
2	October	14	15.95	223.30	<-Hint: =B2*C2
3	November	28	12.00	336.00	
4	December	21	15.95	334.95	
5	4th quarter ebook sales	42	6.00	252.00	
6					
7		105		$1,146.25	
8			Sales Tax	34.39	<-Hint: =D7*.03

Query Tracking with Excel

If you're a freelance writer, use Excel to track submissions, remember when to follow up, track payments, and brainstorm ideas for future articles and markets.

You'll find a free query tracker you can download at my site: www.releaseyourwriting.com/query.html. Help yourself but promise to customize it in Excel for your own preferences and goals. Here's a sample:

You are at best one small project in an editor's production schedule, so the burden to follow up falls to you. Keep good records so you know what you sent, when you sent it, when to follow up, and what editors promised you. You can even cut and paste the text of email messages into Word or Excel so all your documentation is in one place.

I hope this mini-Excel lesson appeals to your orderly mind. Whether you're intrigued or confused, consult the Excel Help files or a book on Excel to learn more.

These are just some examples of how you can use your computer as a partner in the long process of writing a book. When the writing gets tough, don't despair. Don't get tied up. Its only words on a page, the same 26 letters everyone else uses, just rearranged. All you have to do is get them in the right order.

"No tears in the writer,

no tears in the reader."

—Robert Frost

Part 3

The Business of Being a Writer

Chapter 8

Book Marketing and Promotion

If there is any glamour in being a writer, it isn't on the business side. Your responsibilities beyond writing your book seem endless at times. Your computer is your best companion to handle the work.

Writing is becoming more and more a multimedia experience so it really helps to have good computer skills. Don't keep thinking technology will go away. You need some proficiency with the Internet for research, uploading to websites, managing your own site, writing a blog, creating an e-newsletter, and posting audio/video clips.

In Chapter 7, we reviewed word processing tips to cut your work in half by starting with a template for every need: invoices, introduction letters, manuscripts, interview contact sheets and more. We emphasized over 20 features that ease a writer's burden at the computer with macros, shortcuts and other clever tricks.

We've just illustrated the merits of spreadsheets. Use them to track your sales, royalties, sales tax payable, and deductible expenses for your tax return on Schedule C. Spreadsheets are also a good place to start organizing a list of the approvals to quote people, list your sources, and list potential book reviewers.

If you need more power than Excel offers for tracking business income and expenses, use a financial management program like Quicken, Quickbooks, or Microsoft Money to handle bookkeeping chores. Combine that with online bill-payment and you'll cut record keeping down to a few hours a month. If you're writing a book while also freelancing for magazines, you'll be glad if you set up a system to track invoices and payments due on all your work.

Part of financial planning should include goals for your book. Few writers are brave enough to forecast expected sales volume for years 1, 2, and 3, or to chart revenue remaining after marketing expenses. Even when you're writing for the love of it, the reality of tracking and covering costs is valuable information.

Home Office Space

To take your writing seriously, and to get yourself into work mode, it helps to have a distinct professional work area, whether it's a corner of the kitchen, or a table by the sofa.

If you're lucky enough to have a room you can designate as your office, you might consider taking the home office deduction on your taxes. Get full information from the IRS site: www.irs.gov/pub/irs-pdf/p587.pdf. But, a word of caution: If you take the deduction, you have to use the space exclusively for work.

Many people don't realize the home office deduction isn't all it seems, because in the future, when you sell your home, the depreciable basis of the home business space is a factor in the home office deduction. In a year when you don't make a net profit from your writing, you can't take the home office deduction. It's best to consult a financial advisor or accountant for full details before taking the deduction.

Finding Your Target Market

Don't wait until your book is published to begin marketing it. Develop a marketing plan early on and keep modifying it. You already researched your target audience when you decided on the direction of your book. As you think of your readers, pay attention to where those people are and how they shop.

You'll do better with a smaller target, so get specific, and narrow your focus. If your target is single parents, for example, what magazines do they read? Do they attend local lectures and belong to groups? Your goal is not to stalk prospective readers/buyers in parking lots, but to build exposure for your book where they will take notice.

Newsletters and magazine articles are a great place to start. I can't overemphasize the value of collecting email contact information. Start an email newsletter that you send weekly or monthly with tips from your book or related topics of interest. Once your book is out, you'll likely be too busy to pull together a mailing list, so start early.

Write relevant article for periodicals, and adapt your byline to the audience: ".... is author of the upcoming book "Title," to be released this summer. Contact the author for more details."

Marketing Tools

Without a good marketing strategy, you won't sell books. You need an arsenal of self-promotion tools to reach your audience. Here are the ten commandments of visibility:

- Seek book reviews
- Get online links to your work
- Media kit and press release
- Reach beyond "friends & family" to find readers
- Use email for marketing
- Work the web—worldwide
- Create fliers and ads for your book
- Get known in your community
- Submit your book for awards, usually in the year of publication
- Approach book clubs and enter contests.

Book Titles

What makes a good title? Researchers have fun trying to predict successful titles, but no one knows. When you've done your initial audience research and focused on your target reader, revisit your book's title. Does it still fit? Will it attract your target readers?

An effective title research technique is to search www.worldcat.org, the world's largest network of library content and services. See how your proposed book title compares to books and articles on file.

The importance of a good title is always stressed as a critical success factor. But cover design, title visibility and fit on the spine are all elements of a good cover too. Remember, bookstore browsers spend an average of four seconds looking at the front cover and seven seconds studying the back cover before deciding whether to buy your book. Use the back cover to create a powerful promise, and summarize the benefits to the reader. Spiral bound books are difficult to place in stores and libraries, without a proper spine displaying the title.

Networking
Fellow writers and people who support good writing are everywhere. Your local librarian can be a real asset, and people you meet while working on your book

may provide valuable connections. Professional writing organizations such as American Society of Journalists and Authors (ASJA.org), Authors Guild (authorsguild.org), and Freelance Success (freelancesuccess.com), offer advice and support for fellow writers. Annual dues vary by organization, and are worthwhile networking outlets, especially if you feel isolated as a working writer. Some emphasize networking, freelancing, or commercial aspects of publishing. Many have excellent conferences and online groups to keep you involved in the writing community.

Is This Seat Taken?

Attending large conferences can be overwhelming. Get the most out of your time by studying the panels, workshops and agenda in advance. Research the background for the speakers you're interested in hearing. Focus your attention on each session, and take good notes but don't overlook networking opportunities. Sit next to someone you don't know and find out if they've attended the conference before, what kind of writing they do and what other panels they found useful.

When the conference ends, be sure to follow-up with the people you met, and send a thank-you note to anyone who helped you out.

If time and money prevent you from hopping on a plane to attend a conference, don't despair. Online forums and chat groups exist in many forms. If you're new to the idea, start with Google or Yahoo Groups and find a writing group related to your interests. Once you sign in, you can read and participate in the group as little or as much as you wish. Spend a few days reading before you jump in, so you have time to observe the protocols and style. Do it too long, though, by reading and taking information without participating and you'll be considered a lurker. If you like the group, offer ideas of value now and then.

If you need a writing getaway, be sure to check Shaw Guides (shawguides.com) for retreats and workshops worldwide. I'm lucky to live in the Chicago area, home to many fine writing groups. If you're not so lucky, reach out or start one in your area to stay connected. *The Writing Group Book: Creating and Sustaining a Successful Writing Group*, by Lisa Rosenthal is full of ideas for starting local and online writing groups. Consider joining local writing organizations, both for networking opportunities and to support groups who support writers.

Contact Database

A good contact list is a valued resource that will grow as you expand your writing career. Whether you start with a Word address book, an Excel file, Act, or Outlook, get compulsive about tracking every contact you meet, and note their profession. When you need interviews, reviewers, sources, or network connections, the list will be valuable. Keep track of all the editors, agents, sources you've interviewed, networking contacts, fellow writers and leads for future stories. As with your manuscript itself, be diligent about backing up these records to a USB drive, CD or other media.

Wherever you are in the book production process, its not too soon to start your master PR list. Include everyone you know: members of alumni associations, trade groups, local chambers of commerce and other area organizations.

Reviews & Appearances

Line up reviewers, using resources like midwestbookreview.com and ask for reviews from your readers. Remember, traditional media outlets are reluctant to review self-published books, so it's up to you to be resourceful. For my books, I create glossy, color bookmarks that remind readers to go online and write a review after they read the book.

Plan visits to local booksellers as soon as you have your book in hand. If your book is suitable for their customers, most bookstores are very willing to set up a signing event. They will either order your book through Ingram or take books on consignment directly from you.

I know we're all adults here, but remember to be professional when you introduce yourself. Don't stop in to speak to a bookshop owner without copies of your book, business card, a consignment form and marketing materials (bookmarks, postcards, flyers). You can download a sample consignment form at www.releaseyourwriting.com/consign. html. If you really want to impress merchants, memorize your ISBN so you can rattle it off when they look for your book in their database.

While shop owners will often welcome you for an event, they don't have time to do your marketing for you. It will still be up to you to get people to attend your event. Use email invitations, posters and fliers to ensure a good turnout. Have someone take a few pictures of you at events, to build up the publicity section of your site or blog.

Team up with another author for a book signing, at an appropriate venue, perhaps at a café, an outdoor market, or daycare center. Create opportunities to be where your audience is.

Harvest All Contacts

Pass around a sign-up sheet at events, and add those people to your email list, to build your database for future events. Have a printed excerpt or give-away for attendees so no one leaves empty-handed. Word-of-mouth and referrals will broaden interest in your book.

Publicity

Take full advantage of your website, email signature, blog and other accessible online resources to promote your book. Create a full-page color flyer as soon as your final cover art is available and carry it with you everywhere. On the flyer, include your credentials as an author, a brief blurb describing the book, how to purchase, and any endorsements you've received.

Your book enhances your credibility as an expert in your topic, so don't be surprised to find yourself on the local speaker circuit. Having attractive publicity materials, your bio and a strong mailing list will help make your events a success and lead to more invitations to speak and sell books. Even if you're highly motivated to sell books, avoid appearing so. To give audiences a quality experience, promote yourself as a speaker, rather than an author with books to sell.

If you don't have time for these tasks, consider hiring a publicist to book engagements. They often work on a retainer or fee based on activities booked.

Radio
If you can't afford a publicist, use online resources to find opportunities for radio interviews. *Talk Radio for Authors—*

Getting Interviews Across the U.S. and Canada, by Francine Silverman, is a good resource with about 40 categories of radio programs, listing show themes, guest criteria, and contact information. The book includes opinions by radio hosts as to what makes a good or bad radio interview.

Radio-locator.com offers an extensive database of stations, culled from the FCC's public databases. It lists over 500 talk radio stations in the U.S. and Canada, searchable by city and state.

When you get a radio or talk show gig, it's a good idea to submit a few sample questions and answers to steer the appearance toward your talking points and your message.

Internet Promotion

More writers are turning to the Internet for video interviews, podcasts, book trailers, and guest "appearances" on web conferences and reader blogs. It's too early to tell if these online activities will grow in popularity, and more importantly, whether they increase book sales. We will reach the tipping point some day where it may be difficult to attract a quality audience, when few people have time to wade through all the promotions and noise.

For now, though, reach out to these Internet resources and make yourself as visible as you can. This is one market where there are no barriers to entry and the web and blogs are still in a hot growth phase.

Endorsements

If you're not an outgoing person, able to chase Frank McCourt around a cruise ship as a friend of mine did, think of a few people you believe would support the ideas in your book and see its merit. Email or phone the prospects and ask if they will write a blurb for your book. Offer to send the manuscript or a relevant chapter. Make sure your manuscript is in top shape. You don't want to send a bad draft and lose a good endorsement. Advance reading copies are often referred to in the industry as "ARCs."

Remember, marketing never ends. Your book stops selling when you stop selling it. Lucrative sales come from having your book in places of interest to your reader. And that might be niche markets like museums, clubs, reading groups, discount stores, and warehouse clubs. Thinking like an entrepreneur as well as an author will provide more sales channels than bookstores alone.

What else will make you a good marketer? Have a marketing plan that includes at least quarterly visibility in your community. Even introverts need money. Your book won't sell itself, and if your financial plan for the book is not reaching your goal, you've got to market more.

Platform

Now that you've got plenty of ideas for marketing strength, let's look at what the publishing industry calls a "platform." Start by speaking at your local chamber of commerce, attend an expo, and get a booth or table at community events.

Whether you self-publish or go the longer route with an agent and publisher, book marketing is up to you. Having a platform is critical to your visibility and success in book promotion.

Your platform combines your credentials and your outreach:

- Audience
- Experience
- Mailing list
- Website
- Blog exposure
- Book tour availability
- Media and public speaking.

All of these components are essential to promoting your work at the highest level or attracting a publisher, by illustrating your ability to sell books. Your tasks, whether published by a POD service or traditionally, will be to market the book, do author signing events at bookstores, and get your book reviewed. Be creative in exploring free ways to gain visibility.

Large publishers look for authors with a national platform. They want to see your marketing energy and ideas and they want TV and radio poise. Although we're grateful for the opportunities provided by libraries, our local library readings don't count much in the big picture. Platforms build slowly, so start early and climb up little by little.

Publishers print books. They don't manage your career. If you really know your book and know your national or international audience, you are the best person to promote your book. Since the full marketing effort is up to us, many traditional authors switch to self-publishing, so they can control the publishing process, pursue marketing efforts and benefit from higher profits through direct sales, instead of waiting for small royalties.

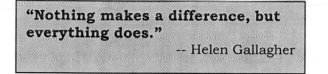

"Nothing makes a difference, but everything does."

-- Helen Gallagher

By that I mean, there isn't a single effort likely to send your book aloft, so don't give up if you get one good review and it doesn't result in stardom. Continue your efforts, and their combined force will create synergy. Since self-published books don't just roll into stores, you need to work at gaining exposure through:

- Pre-launch publicity
- Book launch parties
- Asking stores to carry your book
- Getting reviewed
- Writing articles and getting online listings

📖 Working your platform every
week.

If you have a book coming out soon, start
planning your marketing activities now.
Even one task per week will put you
ahead. Send an email newsletter to sub-
scribers, post a new blog entry, add
events to your website, create external
links, get speaking gigs, send press re-
leases, enter contests, apply for awards,
write columns and articles.

Stay in the public eye by writing op-ed
newspaper pieces and look for news topics related to your book. Visit blogs and
mention your book title in relevant discussions.

Say "Yes" to requests by local TV and radio stations. Use a calendar, like Chase's
Calendar of Events, or an "On this day in
history" website, to tie appearances to
timely events.

However you choose to publish, your
platform is a good predictor of your potential sales. Pay the same attention to
your platform when you self-publish as
you would when working with a mainstream publisher. It's an important tool
in your book's long-term success.

Self-Promotion

Whether you're making bookstore appearances, working a booth, or chasing after book buyers at a trade show, I can't overemphasize the need for projecting a professional image.

You know the basics: Show up in the process and be fully prepared, with business cards, pens, cash, receipt books. Use handouts, such as bookmarks or Q & A cards, a sign-up sheet, entry forms for a drawing. Don't display only the last wrinkly copy of your book. Create an inviting presentation to attract buyers, perhaps leaving a display copy within easy reach and signing a fresh copy for each customer.

Self-marketing means putting your *self* out there. Show that you value yourself and your work with a professional attitude and high-energy spirit. If you're shy, join Toastmasters or practice by speaking to a small group of friends at a home book signing before you stand up in a large bookstore for a reading. Find a way to connect with readers. Audience members often want to hear an author talk about what drew them to the book's idea, or reveal anecdotes, rather than hearing passages from the book. Don't just read from the book and don't model bad examples.

Please don't be:

- ✓ The author who leans against a wall, eyes cast downward, while reading her book to prospective customers.
- ✓ The man who sits in a chair, head down, reading as if he's in his bathroom, when he's in front of a bookstore audience.
- ✓ The person who reads from her book but doesn't have any to sell. "I have to go to Kinko's for more," is not a statement you want to make as an author.
- ✓ The author who discounts her book for no reason—"The price is $12, but you can have it for $5." Unless it fell in a puddle, don't devalue your work.

Online Marketing

While you don't have to become a web master to promote your book, you do need to master the web. Spend time learning what you can do at Amazon, Google, Yahoo and other sites with powerful reach to millions of consumers. Amazon gets most of the attention for online book sales because they're more of a marketing empire than online retailer. They offer many programs for authors, allowing you to cross-link your exposure, and increase revenue potential. Amazon's programs include:

> Amazon connect
> AStore
> Author page
> Author profile
> Listmania
> Search inside the book.

Learn about these features and more at Amazon. Click on "Help" and search for "publishing guides."

A word of caution: Try to keep your efforts proportional to the reward. You're swimming in a very large pool when you swim in the Amazon. It takes a lot of time and effort to master Amazon, and there's no guarantee your efforts will put you on the bestseller list.

Google offers Google Book Search, showing book previews and includes book content in search results. They display full text of out-of-copyright books, or get permission from publishers. The search result can include full text, snippets or a limited preview. Links go to booksellers and libraries. Learn more at www.google.com/intl/en/googlebooks/about.html

Google also has visibility and promotion tools for authors, including AdSense, where you allow Google to place relevant ads on your website or blog and earn a little cash on a pay-per-click basis.

Use Google Alerts for marketing too. Set up a Google Alert to receive a daily email summary of all sites where certain words are mentioned. Be sure to create a Google alert for your book titles, so you'll know whenever the books are mentioned in reviews or on other sites. If you're writing about an industry, trend, or corporation, this technique ensures you don't miss any news.

Create a Google Alert

Enter the topic you wish to monitor.

Search terms:

Type: Comprehensive

How often: once a day

Your email:

Create Alert

Google will not sell or share your email address.

I'll tell you a secret I recently learned about book marketing. I've often seen authors grow disappointed that their book doesn't just magically take off in the market, and they stop their marketing efforts.

Susan Driscoll, President & CEO of iUniverse spoke at an ASJA conference in 2007. She noted: "It can take up to three years for a book to reach peak sales. And what sustains it is word-of-mouth. " So don't let up on your marketing efforts. With the Internet, it's never been easier.

Handling Information Overload
With exponential growth in the number of websites, we won't easily win the battle for controlling our time and efficiency online. There's always another great site,

another new place to post or read about topics of interest.

We don't have time to keep up with the wealth of information, so the best recourse is to keep a tight list of folders in your browser's Bookmarks or Favorites, and file the desired sites diligently. Use folders within your bookmarks for topics and categories, or keep a folder called "To Read" or "Priority" so you can get back to the best of them.

Print a copy of the bookmarks when you're doing research, but back up and purge the file regularly. Some power web users create a page, even in Excel or Word, of hyperlinks, save it as a web page, (.html), and use it as a home page, so bookmarks are always at hand.

Effective Web Searching
Finding good information online is not a function of which search tool you use, but how well you ask the questions.

What's your favorite search tool? Chances are you prefer Google. People love it but it's not always the best tool for the job. Google was the top choice for over 53 percent of web searchers as of

January, 2007, according to Nielsen/NetRatings. But a good fit depends on your need and there are other tools to explore for effective online research. Because Google search results are based on the number of links to sites, i.e., popularity, its results often have little to do with relevance.

If you're committed to Google, spend some time learning advanced search techniques to deliver better results. Use Google Scholar for relevant research on scholarly topics at scholar.google.com.

The next time you're doing a web search, explore a few other tools. You'll widen your knowledge base, support a dynamic market, and prevent the dominance of a sole player. Here are a few powerful search tools with advanced benefits for effective online searches.

A9 from Amazon.com includes media columns, images and blogs in search results, without having to do an "advanced" search. The toolbar lets you leave notes on web pages, sort of like bookmarks, and lets you search your history files and bookmarks. Users can search at: "generic.a9.com" to avoid having their browser information collected.

Answers.com You may already use this site as a homework helper for the family. It searches authoritative sites, not popular sites, bringing you research from Columbia University Press, Merriam Webster, MarketWatch and more. It uses a new paradigm that brings instant information, with topic-based responses, not just links to where the search term may or may not exist. Treasures such as science and technology achievements are categorized by year, back to the 17th century.

Clusty.com is my personal favorite to find anything fast. It clusters results from several search engines and sorts by topic. A click on "advanced" also expands your search to include news sources including Reuters, *The New York Times*, CNN, *USA Today, Washington Post* and BBC News. You can cluster your search to return from 100 up to 500 results, all sorted by category.

HotBot.com was a mainstay of search tools long before Google. Now that it's turbocharged with content from four of the best search engines on the Web: Google, FAST, Inktomi, and Teoma, it can give you more results than a single Google search.

Info.com is even better because it provides results from 14 different search engines and directories, including Google, Ask, Yahoo, and more. Info.com's news service integrates news feed from Topix.net, to continuously monitor breaking news from more than 7,000 sources.

Teoma.com is a favorite of researchers because it's focus is relevance. It's available through Hotbot as well as directly at teoma.com. Teoma returns search results based on popularity, like Google, but does so with a subject-specific filter to determine relevance. Advanced tools at Teoma include narrowing your selection by exact phrase, page location, geographic region, and date range.

Privacy Issues

If you install free desktop search bars, be aware the provider is collecting at least basic web behavior information from you. Search engines, like many online programs we use, collect some personal information including Internet addresses, connection information, browser type, operating system, the path of clicks to and from websites, and pages you've viewed.

Writers' Website Basics: Mini-Boot Camp
Websites are common today, not only for business, but also for fundraising, family, friends, hobbies, and to remove isolation for the self-employed and special interest groups. While not everyone needs a website, it is an affordable place to experiment, express your ideas and share information, gaining visibility far beyond your local community. Most web hosts offer website creation templates you can use to create a website.

The first step is to buy a unique domain name, which costs only about $20/year. Then find a host to keep your site running on a computer accessible worldwide. Professional hosting costs less than $10/month and includes an email address and plenty of storage space for files and photos. In addition to the unique stature of a domain name, once you have a domain, it becomes your brand name online.

Think of a domain as a pen name, if you wish to publish a book on a topic unrelated to your primary career. Be advised, though, that anyone can do a "whois" lookup and learn your true name and address at Network Solutions: (www.networksolutions.com/whois/index.jsp). Use the "whois" database to check on the status of your domain name and see the expiration date, and search the database to find names similar to yours. Avoid choosing a domain name that is awkward to spell, type, or is easily confused with other sites.

Choosing a domain name is just a little easier than naming a baby. It takes a lot of thought to come up with a domain name that's easy to spell and remember.
The .com domain extension is the most logical choice for commercial sites, since .org is intended for non-profits, .edu for schools, and sub-domains such as .info, .tv, .biz really haven't taken off.

If your book title stands apart from others, and/or it's your only book, consider using that for a domain name. I did that with this book, choosing www.releaseyourwriting.com because I already have three other websites only tangentially related to writing. But if yours is one of many books you've written or you have other elements of your platform to convey, think of a broader domain name that is less specific and can represent your entire portfolio of work.

Email tip: Route all your email to your domain name, no matter who your underlying email provider is. That way, when you change Internet providers, or move and your email address changes, you let the new address forward email to your domain. The change is transparent to the public. You can print your domain name and email address on your literature without fear of having to change it. As a side benefit, instead of advertising your mail host, your email address matches your website, and is part of your identity. As an example, I bought the domain, www.cclarity.com in 1996, and I've had the same public email address, Helen@cclarity.com, more than ten years even though I've changed Internet providers three times.

There are no actual rules in the wild, wild web, but you won't attract visitors if your website and blog don't offer something of value to readers. My goal is always to write a site well and then reduce it by half. Choose graphics carefully, and pay attention to font size and color. Use adequate contrast, not orange on yellow or grey on black. Make links large enough to click on the first try. Offer a way to get back to the home page, and to navigate within sections of your site.

For a new site:

If you don't have a website yet, create one this year. Don't wait until you suddenly have extra time or know exactly what you want. Like designing a new kitchen, you won't really know what you want until you start putting the plan together.

If you're building a new site, look at other sites to determine what you like. At a minimum you'll probably want to start with:

About the book
About the author
How to purchase
Contact info

Later you can add more pages, such as sample chapters, testimonials, a signup form for e-newsletters, online credit card orders, and an event list. Use inbound and outbound links to increase your search visibility.

If you have an existing site:

1. Critically evaluate the content.
2. What do you like on your site?
3. Is the material fresh and relevant?
4. What traffic or hits do you get? Find out through your web host.
5. What is your goal for your site?
6. Does it get the results you want?

Start promoting your book through your own website or blog right away. As you develop more marketing ideas, you can expand the site, but start, even if you don't have all your ideas in place, so you can use the Internet to reach your audience.

Keep it fresh:

Add new material to encourage return visitors to your site, either event updates, photos, or news about your topic. Here are ten website content suggestions to get you started:

1. Link to your blog

2. Newsletter
3. Email subscription
4. Comment area
5. Calendar of events
6. Relevant news
7. Surveys
8. Photos
9. Handy downloads and tips
10. Link to a network of experts

Search Engine Savvy

It's a big world out there. You won't rise to the top in search engines without work and luck. Rather than seeking top placement in search engines worldwide, consider reaching your target market. Remember you wrote your book for a specific audience. Strive to reach them effectively by being visible both online and offline.

Links

When search engines prowl the web, creating listings for sites, they look for lots of hyperlinks and depth of content. On a badly designed page, users have to 'scrub' the page, rubbing the mouse all over to determine where the live hyperlink are hiding. Boost your visibility in search engines by linking to articles and relevant reference material. Be careful not to send people away from your site by linking to too many external sites and don't place external links at the top of your site. You might lose visitors before they've had a chance to find what they want on your site.

Stand Out From the Crowd
With over 5,000 new websites created each week, it's not easy to be found by our target audiences. How can you separate yourself and rise above the crowd?

Building traffic to your site, like building buzz for your book, will come from word-of-mouth and referrals. To catch the attention of your audience, try this trick: View sites similar to yours and click "View/Page Source" in your web browser. Up near the top of the programming code you should see that site's list of keywords.

Here's a small metatag example:
```
<HTML>
<HEAD>
<TITLE>Your Site Title</TITLE>
<META NAME="description"
CONTENT="American history. Ore-
gon author of (book title) and his-
```

torian offers workshops, free e-
news, blog and excerpts. ">
<META NAME="keywords"
CONTENT="Oregon author, mem-
oir, (book title) (author name), his-
torian, journalist, national workshop leader.">
</HEAD>

The format is specific to HTML (hypertext markup) language, but you can use
a free metatag generator online to create
the code, (see www.ineedhits.com). You,
or your web wizard, then paste it as a
"tag" on your web pages. Make sure to
use your relevant keywords in page titles,
and in the first few words of your de-
scription. That's what people see when
they view your site in a search engine
listing. There is no magic way to get
listed at the top of search engines.

Once you have keywords in place, use a
submission service or manual labor to
list your site in search engines and
community sites, specific to your book's
market. Search engines work by crawling
the web, reading metatags, looking for
relevant content and indexing it. The
more your site is updated, the more inbound and outbound links you have, the

more topics it finds to categorize, and the more places you'll show up.

Most website owners appreciate being cross-linked, which aids web visibility for both parties. Be sure to ask permission before creating a link to someone else's site. The exponential growth from cross-links can result in phenomenal traffic for your site, as long as you offer value to your visitors.

You can also pay for positioning, bidding a price at search engines, which might place your site at or near the start of a topic list. Appearing in search results doesn't mean your site is a relevant match to your audience. Again, think of your target audience and the best way to reach them, rather than spanning the universe, hoping your target audience will notice. Keep your goal in mind, and if that is to sell books, just having a website appear in non-specific searches won't likely generate business by itself.

Three steps to web success:

1. Keep your site in good
   health. Check it frequently
   for missing images, broken
   links, or outdated pages.
2. Use links. Search engines
   love links. That's the origin
   of the "web" concept.
3. And, content is still king.
   Compelling information
   worthy of the reader's time
   will increase your site's ef-
   fectiveness.

Best Website Strategies

Design is critical but, especially with
your first website, you have to experience
the site live to know how it flows and
what you really want. So I don't recommend you spend thousands of dollars on
a web designer when you're starting out.
Create the concept for the site yourself or
with a coach at your side.

If you're not sure how to start, create a
prototype of your site on paper. Lay out
what you want on each page, decide on
appropriate page names, and think about
which pages should link to others. Pay

attention to page titles because they become the name people see when they
print or bookmark a page. You don't
want a page called "ebdd147.html," if it's
actually "About the Author."

Create your site with a tool you can use
easily, so you can make changes without
incurring web designer fees. You can
have an attractive design with text areas
you can update using a tool like Macromedia Contribute, Adobe GoLive, Microsoft Publisher or a good web editor.
FrontPage is not recommended because
Microsoft stopped selling it. You can even
create a website in word processing software, such as Word. Create your text and
graphics, and then choose "File/Save as
web page" or ".html." A useful utility program called File Transfer Protocol (FTP) is
a free download. With it you can send
your site's pages and images from your
computer to the web host. It's as easy as
sending an email.

Another clever benefit of a website is
storage space. When you purchase web
hosting, you usually receive several giga-
bytes (GB) of storage space. It's a pass-
word-protected space where you can upload files and make them available to the
public. You might want to load product

photos or articles, scanned images, voice or video clips and documents related to a specific interest. The files needn't be accessible through your site's navigation scheme, just available to you in subfolders. Give out the address to a subfolder if you want a colleague to review material before you post it, or give people a sneak preview of a new project. By knowing how to upload pages and files, using FTP, you can also use that space as a virtual closet, storing archives and extra backups of your manuscript for safekeeping. As long as you don't make a web link to a page, you're the only one who can access those files.

Invite web visitors by printing your web address on everything you do: your email signature, envelopes, invoices, business cards and ads. If your site name is short and easy to convey, include it on your outgoing voicemail message.

Blogs

We've made enough casual reference to blogs so by now, you're probably wondering if you should have one. If a website is more complex than you need, you can create a blog for free. And, updating it is as easy as sending an email. Don't overlook a blog as a way to gain exposure for your writing and your web site. It's also an outlet for you to post your ideas and stimulate discussions.

One drawback to blogs is they are generally chronological. You can get around that by using links to organize the content but it's not a perfect replacement for the depth that a website offers. It's a nice counterpoint, though, easy to update, always fresh and topical.

Why Have a Blog?
1. It's free and such an easy way to gain presence online.
2. It bears your contact info or a link back to your site.
3. It spurs dialog.
4. You can quickly convey information to your audience.
5. It's leads to more exposure for your work.
6. As a writer, you won't likely get hired to write for a blog if you don't have one.

Perhaps the best way to pull yourself into blog culture is to start one. Free blogs are available through Blogger.com (owned by Google), LiveJournal.com and

WordPress. Typepad starts at $4.95/month. Once you sign up, you create your first blog post, and then return to it when your muse beckons. Blog posts are generally short, contain links of interest, and invite comments. Styles are far from conventional, so anything goes.

Publishing industry executives and agents watch blogs to spot trends, see writing samples, and sometimes approach writers for a book deal. They also prowl blog search engines, like technorati.com to see what's new. I know of several "blog-to-book" deals, including Wandering Scribe, the blog of a homeless girl in England. She lived in her car and maintained an anonymous blog during public library visits. A BBC reporter read the blog, drove out to find her, and she is no longer homeless and unknown. Anya Peter's book *Abandoned* now has a sales ranking near the top 1,000 at Amazon UK (amazon.co.uk).

Blog writing generally bears little resemblance to a daily diary. Thoughtful essays, pondering issues and topics only tangentially related to your main theme are all allowed. Visit blogs and you'll see an expansive range of work and play.

Be careful, though, about how much of your book you post online. Many publishers require exclusive right to print or post your work. While most writers' guidelines were written years before the Internet boom, use caution before posting your work on public sites and blogs. It can be difficult to remove your work from the web once it gets in circulation, and once you're under contract, publishers want to control access to your work. You may, for example, be permitted to display your book cover on your own website, but not to offer excerpts, distribution or online sales.

We see increasing synergy between websites and blogs, between author books and blogs, and between blogs and book deals. Remember, agents and editors read blogs, and they sign clients if they see potential for a book and a loyal audience. If you need another reason to start a blog, it's a great way to exercise your writing muscle.

Web Writing
If your writing extends beyond your website and blog, think pithy. Writing articles, doing online interviews, and promoting your book may take you to the

web, where the writing is lean. If you use the web, you're already acquainted with some of the differences. Certainly, for ease of reading, text is broken up into more paragraphs, calling attention to details with variations in font and spacing. To fit limited attention span and space, most web writing is brief—not as short as a fortune cookie, but brief. Web writing makes use of hypertext, to let restless readers move ahead, jump back, and avoid boredom with on-screen reading.

While it's true this makes the web an imperfect venue for your best prose, it's also a powerful way to reach a wide audience and draw interest to your topic and your writing.

Chapter 9

Keep Your Book Alive

If you think writing a book takes a long time, it's nothing compared to marketing it. Books don't sell themselves. It takes lots of marketing power, either through large budgets funded by publishers, or your own grassroots marketing efforts. Either way, it takes a lot of time, exposure, and a polished message to sell your book.

Turn to this marketing section when you need ideas for new avenues to stimulate sales.

The primary rule: Always have your elevator pitch ready.

Example:
Computer Ease is like a marriage counselor for you and your computer.

Release Your Writing helps authors succeed in publishing books and navigating the marketing maze.

Putting Money into Marketing

It's time to talk money again. Many authors do well without investing a lot in marketing and advertising. You can find hundreds of websites to promote your book, as we covered earlier. But you might want to put some serious money into marketing if you know that's the best way to reach your specific target audience.

A *Business Week* article reported 51 percent of authors surveyed in 2005 invested personal funds in marketing their book.

1. The amount authors personally invested in their books ranged from under $1,000 to $150,000, with a median investment amount of $4,500.
2. Authors who hired "outside help" sold 10,000 copies of their first book and earned royalties of $55,000, compared to 4,500 copies sold and royalties of $25,000 for authors who depended solely on the efforts of their publishers. (Publishers Weekly)
3. Most effective marketing tactic: Using the Internet

4. Second most effective marketing tactic: generating press in trade publications related to the non-fiction topic.

5. Book signings were not considered effective.

6. Authors who hired reputable firms to promote their book earned higher royalties.

7. Authors said there were many indirect benefits to marketing their books rather than straight sales.

Source: *Business by the Book*, Business Week, 4/12/06, Karen E. Klein, and *Documenting the Value of Marketing*, Publishers Weekly, 4/24/06, Jim Milliot

Contests and Awards

Book marketing is no time to be shy. Be confident about entering contests and competing for awards. Maybe your book won't win, but it sure won't win if it's in a box under your desk. *Writers Digest* has a self-published book award yearly and those self-published authors might still be searching for an agent if self-publishing wasn't a viable option. Pay attention to contest fees, and weigh your odds. You can find many awards and contests with very low entry fees.

Online Markets

And while many web users grow insular about how much of the world they explore online, the web is an ever-expanding universe. Don't neglect overseas markets. I often have book sales through Amazon UK, and have sold a few to people in Italy, Peru and other distant places.

Ebooks serve a special niche, giving people instant access to our books at low cost with no shipping expense or lengthy delays.

Posting articles in online magazines (ezines) lets you share excerpts from your book and gain exposure. Most include a byline where you can plug your book.

Media Kit

Whether you're attending a conference or stopping in at a local bookshop, keep your media kit handy. You'll make a better impression by showing you are serious about your book and your audience.

At a minimum, a media kit should contain a color copy of your book jacket and your contact information. Include a press release, your bio, endorsements, and a list of other upcoming events at cafes or bookstores.

Catalogs and Book Clubs

With about 15,000 catalogs in print, offering gifts, inspiration and impulse purchases, you might find a good match for your book. How do you get in to catalogs and book clubs? Call the catalog publisher for the buyer's name, and ask for submission information. They will generally want to see a sample book, and want your publisher contact information, as well as your current marketing plan. If the catalog is for a book club, they may want to change the cover and do a special print run. You don't need to send sales history. They have access to that information. These firms work way ahead of publication, so make inquiries early.

Book clubs can be gold for you. Approach organizations such as Target.com's BookMarked (bookmarked.target.com). Books-A-Million, Inc. has four book clubs, heavily promoted online at www.booksamillion.com. In addition to a general club, they have Faith, Literary and Teen book clubs.

Podcasts

As technology evolves, more people turn to the Internet for marketing via social networking sites. Even major magazines and publishers now have pages on myspace.com to broaden their exposure.

Simon & Schuster, Inc. recently partnered with TurnHere.com to develop BookVideos.tv, a "social media video site." If book buyers respond to this new outreach, we may see fewer in-store author events, and surely these firms expect the book sales to continue through interaction with the BookVideos.tv site.

You can create your own book blogs and author interviews as podcasts. Virtual book tours offer you great opportunities for visibility, usually at no cost. Do they work? As I said earlier: Nothing makes a difference, but everything does. It doesn't hurt to put yourself out there to take advantage of low cost or free marketing opportunities. It might make a difference. Firms like Tricom Publicity, Inc. offer a program called "Author in your Pocket." Tricom tapes interviews with authors at festivals and events, and people can listen to interviews, mixed with attractive graphics. As people get busier and bus-

176

ier, I suspect the limited time and attention of potential readers may make these projects untenable.

There is still room in the world for audio books, although the market for self-published books is small. Most audio books are now available via download to burn on a CD or in MP3 audio format.

Now that you're armed with self-publishing knowledge and manuscript preparation tips, you're probably eager to get back to your writing and your book publishing goals. You can return to this chapter any time you want to consider your marketing options, get ideas for promoting your book, and keep your book alive. It may seem like an unending task, but if you focus on ideas that fit where you are now, you can handle new challenges as they come along.

Pre-publication Checklist	
Print a copy for your use at www.releaseyourwriting.com/prepub.html	
	Author bio and photo
	Binder to show at bookstores
	Binding, font, paper color
	Edition
	Fact sheet
	Graphics

	ISBN & barcode (POD firm provides)
	Packet for media
	Press release
	Price
	Promo items: bookmarks, notepads
	Publication date
	Publicity plan
	Sample pages
	Subject/category
	Ten word description, elevator pitch
	Title page and cover art

Action Plan Upon Publication

Break out the champagne. You've launched your book! Now launch that stellar marketing program. Use 21st century strategies to spread your wings online with blogs, podcasts, social networking sites, listing your book at Amazon, Barnes & Noble (bn.com), Google and dozens of ebook sites. Keep your website updated and give people a reason to visit it often.

Remember, iUniverse's President & CEO, Susan Driscoll notes it can take up to three years for a book to reach its full potential. Yet, many authors stop marketing after the initial book buzz. Driscoll notes that word-of-mouth, the top-selling factor for most books, takes that long to reach a peak. So don't plan to sit back and wait for future sales if you're not actively promoting the book. As the publishing adage goes: "Your book stops selling when you stop selling it."

Keep working the web. Do one thing a month, every month, to increase your exposure. Although your book will be on major online retail sites, you can leverage the broad reach of the web by cross listing, and linking to your book in all reviews you post online for colleagues and friends.

Seek reviews; get in stores online and across the country. Write articles in newsletters, magazines and newspapers to get press. Work your affiliations by joining organizations that will increase your exposure and let you learn from others in your field.

And remember to support your fellow writers. Like supporting independent bookstores, if we expect them to be around for us, we must also commit to supporting them. If you go to a bookstore to hear authors speak, buy their books. Don't ask if the books are sold online so you can save a couple dollars. As an author, you know how hard that person worked to bring you the book. Treat fellow writers with kindness.

The publishing industry is changing, and the new business model includes plenty of room for small presses and self-published authors to succeed as mainstream authors. Don't be dissuaded by lack of response from an agent or publisher. When you believe in your book, you will find a way. As Jan Phillips says in *Marry Your Muse,* about writing her book:

> "As I write this now, I have no evidence that these words will see the light of day, and yet I give it my time because I believe in it. Because it calls me from my bed. It wakes me up. It holds me and does not let me go
>
> This compilation of words, images, dreams, this piece of art, now with its own life, calls on me to believe in it. And I do. And when you read it one day, you will see for yourself how it happens. The piece starts with an impulse to share, builds into a body of work, takes on its own energy, and finds its way to the world."

We're all so lucky to be writers. We have the curiosity and desire to explore our own thoughts, and express them publicly. By writing, we constantly test our-selves to learn what we know. Whether writing is a hobby, passion, or career, it turns life into a remarkable journey.

Release _your_ writing, and enjoy the re-wards of sharing your work with the world.

"The love of learning, the sequestered nooks,
and all the sweet serenity of books."

Henry Wadsworth Longfellow
1807-1882

Appendix: Writing Resources

Note: The ebook version of *Release Your Writing* contains clickable hyperlinks to all these resources. Order an instant download at www.virtualbookworm.com.

About Self-Publishing
A list of book publishers, small, large, and specialty markets
www.readersread.com/booklinks/bookpublishers/

Dan Poynter's site for cooperative marketing programs, education and advocacy within the publishing industry
www.parapub.com/sites/para/

Realistic, practical information on self-publishing from Jacqueline Simonds'
www.creativemindspress.com/printing.htm#POD percent20v percent20offset

SPAN: Small Publishers of North America
www.spannet.org/

Ebooks
Blueprint Books
www.blueprintbooks.com

Books on Board, www.booksonboard.com

Ebook Mall, www.ebookmall.com

Ebookstand, www.ebookstand.com

Ebook Readers
Adobe Acrobat Reader,
www.adobe.com/products/acrobat/
adobepdf.html

Microsoft Reader,
www.microsoft.com/reader

Ergonomics
Carpal Tunnel prevention exercises
www.carpaltunnelsite.com/portal/carpal
-tunnel-hand-exercise.html

Carpal Tunnel research
www.personalmd.com

Healthy Computing
www.healthycomputing.com

Marketing, Promotion and Research
Authors & Speakers Network
www.authorsandspeakersnetwork.com

Boomer Women

www.boomerwomenspeak.com

Digital-Women, digital-women.com

Google's Writers Resources
www.google.com/Top/Arts/Writers_Resources

Internet Resources for Writers
www.Internet-resources.com/writers

Open Directory Project,
www.dmoz.org/Arts/Writers_Resources/
Publishing

Nuts & Bolts
Book cover designs
www.bookcoverexpress.com

R. R. Bowker, ISBN resource
www.isbn.org/standards/home/isbn/us
/isbnqa.asp

All about ISBN's, www.book-publishers-
compared.com/isbn_international_
standard_book_number.asp

Speech Recognition
Dragon NaturallySpeaking,
www.nuance.com/naturallyspeaking

Microsoft Windows Speech Recognition
For Windows XP:
support.microsoft.com/kb/306901
For Vista:
www.microsoft.com/enable/products/
windowsvista/speech.aspx

Microsoft clipart usage license
www.office.microsoft.com/en-
us/tou.aspx?wzLLCC=en-
US&iA=82&wzA=&iD=82&wzD=#HowYou
MayUseTheService

The Tech Psychologist, Dr. Jeanne Beckman
www.techpsychologist.com

Publishing Advice
John Kremer's personal filing cabinet
www.bookmarket.com/files.htm

Mark Levine, *The Fine Print*
www.book-publishers-compared.com
/self_publishing_companies.asp

Marilyn & Tom Ross Self Publishing
Resources
www.selfpublishingresources.com

Self-pub FAQ (frequently asked questions)
www.writing-world.com/selfpub/FAQ.shtml

Recommended Reading

There are hundreds of good books geared to writers and writing advice. Read 'em all, if you have time. Here are a few of my favorites.

A Writers Paris: A Guided Journey for the Creative Soul, Eric Maisel (Writer's Digest Books, 2005)

The Forest for the Trees, Betsy Lerner (Pan Books, 2002)

Getting Things Done: The Art of Stress-Free Productivity, David Allen (Penguin, 2001)

Marry Your Muse: Making a Lasting Commitment to Your Creativity, Jan Phillips (Quest Books, 1997)

Pen on Fire: A Busy Woman's Guide to Igniting the Writer Within, Barbara DeMarco-Barrett (Harcourt, 2004)

Putting Your Passion into Print: Get Your Book Published Successfully!
by Arielle Eckstut, David Sterry (Workman Publishing, 2005)

Self-Publishing Manual: How to Write, Print and Sell Your Own Book, Dan Poynter (Para Publishing, 2007-16th ed.)

Six-Figure Freelancing, Kelly James-Enger (Random House, 2005)

Thinking Like Your Editor: How to Write Great Serious Nonfiction and Get It Published, Susan Rabiner, Alfred Fortunato (W.W. Norton & Co., 2003)

The Writing Group Book, ed. Lisa Rosenthal (Chicago Review Press, 2003)

Review Sources
Compulsive Reader,
www.compulsivereader.com

Foreword Magazine,
www.forewordmagazine.com

Get Book Reviews,
www.getbookreviews.com

Midwest Book Review,
www.midwestbookreview.com

Specialty book distributors/wholesalers

Anderson News, LLC
www.andersonnews.com

Bookazine Co. Inc
www.bookazine.com

Hudson Booksellers
www.hudsongroup.com

Midpoint Trade Books
www.midpointtrade.com

The Paradies Shops, Inc.
www.theparadiesshops.com

Glossary

Acronym/Term	Definition
Bitmap	Image comprised of dots-per-inch
BMP	Bitmap image file
DPI	Dots-per-inch
Ebook	Digital edition of printed matter
FAQ	Frequently asked questions
FTP	File transfer protocol
Galley	Publishing term for page proofs of manuscript
GB	Gigabyte: one billion bytes of data
GIF	Image type: graphical interface format
HTML	Hyper-text markup language
HTTP	Hyper-text transmission protocol
ISBN	International book standard number
JPG	Image type: Joint Photographic Group standard
MB	Megabyte: one million bits of data
MP3	MPEG—digital music standard
OCR	Optical character recognition
PDF	Portable document format

RSS	Really simple syndication
TIF or TIFF	Tagged image file format: for images: fax, scans
URL	Uniform resource locator

INDEX

194

Acknowledgements

I live in a large community of writers in the Chicago area. Over my career, my professional world blended into a personal life rich with friends who are lovers of words, technology and the incessant Irish need to gather and chat over a pot of tea. Bless them all for listening to my ideas and tolerating my enthusiasm for getting things done. Their support provides a gateway for me to help others get their ideas out into the world.

I am forever grateful to Jerry Enenstein, for everything he is and continues to be, and to Peg Miller, who wears many hats in my life as sister, artist, and friend with a very big heart. Marguerite O'Connor shares the writing fever with me, and is a joy and inspiration on our mutual journey. I thank her for editing my work softly, on lavender paper. Thanks to my clients who give me time off now and then to write. And, of course, to fellow writers who publish their books, giving life to words and words to people.

About the author

Always a word lover, Helen Gallagher was lured to computers because they had an Escape key. Since launching Computer Clarity in 1996, she has been teaching and solving problems for users from 9 to 90. As a consultant, she shares her philosophy and computer confidence with over 250 clients.

In her earlier book, *Computer Ease*, Helen serves as marriage counselor between you and your computer. Here, in *Release Your Writing*, she takes on the mystery of the publishing world, and makes book publishing accessible to all authors. *Release Your Writing* covers everything from research and writing to formatting a manuscript and choosing a publishing method, traditional or self-published.

A freelance writer for ten years, Helen writes on business, technology and travel, and is a national speaker. She is a member of ASJA as well as other national and local associations that support writers and technology. Helen has a B.A. in Finance from Elmhurst University, and lives in Glenview, Illinois.

Contact: Helen@cclarity.com,
www.releaseyourwriting.com

Printed in the United States
106856LV00001B/22/A